SOCIAL
MEDIA BUSINESS

JULIAN DELPHIKI

SOCIAL MEDIA BUSINESS

Define your social strategy, start selling on social media and expand your business in China

- Julian Delphiki -

Social Media Business / Julian Delphiki – 1st Edition

ISBN 979-8642843048

INDEX

PART I
SOCIAL MEDIA STRATEGY

INTRODUCTION

I t is almost guaranteed that you are already familiar with social media, and are using it to chat with friends, share pictures, and perhaps even in your work. But in these pages, we are going to guide you through everything you need to know about social media: the latest trends and developments and how to get the most out of it for your brand, campaigns, and activity. In this first chapters, we are going to explore what exactly social media is and how many of the brands you are familiar with are already using it, and introduce the trends and issues which you, as a brand and as an individual, need to be aware of.

STATE OF SOCIAL MEDIA IN 2024

Currently, social media is becoming less social than ever. One of the primary reasons for this shift is the increasing focus of social media platforms on content from influencers rather than connections with friends.

Initially, social media platforms were designed to foster connections between individuals, allowing people to share updates, photos, and thoughts with their friends and family. The core idea was to create a virtual space where social interactions could thrive, transcending geographical boundaries. However, over time, the landscape of social media has evolved significantly.

Today, the algorithms driving these platforms prioritize content that generates the most engagement, which often comes from influencers and popular content creators rather than personal connections. Influencers, with their large followings and professionally curated content, are seen as more likely to keep users engaged and on the platform longer. This shift in focus means that users are increasingly exposed to a steady stream of sponsored posts, product placements, and lifestyle content from influencers.

While this type of content can be entertaining and sometimes informative, it often comes at the expense of genuine social interaction. Instead of seeing updates from friends about their daily lives, users are more likely to encounter polished and commercially-driven posts from influencers. This can create a sense of disconnection, as the original purpose of staying in touch with personal contacts is overshadowed by a constant barrage of influencer content.

Another reason for the decreasing social nature of social media is the increasing prevalence of product-related content. Social media platforms are evolving into powerful sales channels, incorporating features such as live streaming shopping. While these developments enhance the platforms' commercial capabilities, they further diminish the focus on social connections.

Social media's transformation into a marketplace is evident in the growing number of advertisements, sponsored posts, and direct shopping options integrated into the user experience. Platforms like Instagram, Facebook, and TikTok have introduced features that allow users to shop directly from posts, stories, and live streams. Live streaming shopping events, where influencers or brands showcase products in real-time and interact with potential buyers, are becoming increasingly popular. These features leverage social media's interactive nature to drive sales, creating a seamless shopping experience within the app.

However, the emphasis on commercial content often comes at the expense of personal interactions. As users scroll through their feeds, they encounter a higher volume of product promotions and sales pitches rather than updates from friends and family. This shift can make the social media experience feel more like browsing a digital catalog than engaging in a community of personal connections.

The commercialization of social media also affects how users engage with content. Instead of participating in conversations or sharing personal experiences, users are more likely to interact with branded content through likes, shares, or purchases. This transactional form of engagement can lead to a more superficial interaction with the platform, reducing the depth and quality of social interactions.

Moreover, the constant exposure to product-related content can contribute to consumer fatigue and overwhelm. Users may find themselves inundated with targeted ads and promotional posts, which can detract from the enjoyment and relaxation that social media once provided. This environment can make it harder for users to find and connect with the personal content they initially came to the platform for.

Finally, the emergence of virtual influencers could significantly disrupt the nature of the content and profiles that users are consuming on social media. Virtual influencers, or computer-generated characters that act as influencers, are becoming increasingly prevalent. These digital personas are crafted with advanced technologies, allowing them to interact with followers, endorse products, and engage in promotional activities just like human influencers. However, their rise brings a new set of challenges to the social media landscape.

Virtual influencers are created with precision, often embodying idealized features and lifestyles that are meticulously curated by their creators. They are immune to many of the issues that human influencers face, such as scandals, fatigue, or inconsistencies, which makes them appealing to brands seeking reliable and controllable marketing tools. As a result, these virtual figures can dominate social media feeds with content that is consistently polished and on-brand.

However, the prevalence of virtual influencers, more on that later, can further erode the authenticity and relatability of social media. Unlike human influencers who share their personal experiences, struggles, and successes, virtual influencers are entirely fictional.

This lack of genuine human connection can make interactions with their content feel superficial and contrived. Users may find it harder to connect on an emotional level with a digital persona, which can diminish the sense of community and real-life connection that social media once provided.

Social media channel will be redefined not as much as the users want but what the platforms needs -more data, more walled gardens, more revenue from advertisers or sales fees-.

THE RISE OF VIRTUAL INFLUENCERS

Traditionally, companies have often utilized animated or illustrated mascots—such as Tony the Tiger, the Jolly Green Giant, and the Geico Gecko—as the face of their brand. These characters have proven successful, and with the rise of artificial intelligence and the growing influence of real-life digital influencers, it's no surprise that businesses are now exploring virtual AI influencers to represent their brands.

These computer-generated characters or avatars, designed to resemble humans and powered by algorithms, can interact with users on social media, create content, and endorse products or services. This trend has gained traction among brands looking for innovative ways to engage audiences and leverage influencer marketing. Seventeen members of the Forbes Agency Council provide insights into how AI influencers might revolutionize brand representation.

The following insights, while sometimes contradictory, suggest that the impact of virtual influencers is still unfolding, but they are undeniably already part of the marketing landscape.

Success with AI influencer marketing will mirror the success found in real influencer marketing. Brands that align their AI influencer campaigns with audience interests and maintain their core identity will thrive. Those chasing novelty may not fare as well.

AI influencers, particularly in fashion, have shown promise. However, success requires more than creating unique characters. Storylines, character development, and creativity are essential to sustain engagement and impact.

Integrating AI influencers as the "face" of a brand requires careful consideration. While AI promises significant business impacts, akin to the internet's evolution, its timing in marketing conflicts with the demand for authenticity. Employing AI influencers can be effective, but it must be done thoughtfully and not merely for convenience.

AI's greatest advantage is its ability to be customized. AI influencers can be tailored to appeal to any demographic and can be quickly adjusted to target different audiences. This level of personalization surpasses that of traditional influencers, offering more precise and consistent customer engagement.

AI mascots could serve as advanced animated spokespeople, capable of real-time interaction with consumers through voice activation, complete with realistic body and facial expressions. The potential for interactivity with AI brand mascots is exciting. Expect AI mascots that can interact with audiences via chat or augmented reality, merging brand spokesperson and customer service roles into one.

While AI influencers can rapidly create, test, and scale strategies, this speed can also lead to challenges in maintaining authenticity and alignment with the brand, making it hard to build a consistent presence.

There will inevitably be AI-influencer failures, which might even become a source of amusement, like Wendy's social media team poking fun at these missteps. Some brands will experiment with AI influencers, but many may abandon the approach, realizing that real people prefer trusting other real people over digital mascots. Some fashion and lifestyle brands might find success, but they will be exceptions.

Time will tell if AI influencers will prevail or if people will prefer connecting with real humans. AI influencers offer dynamic experiences but lack the long-standing emotional and nostalgic connections that traditional mascots have with audiences. Building similar connections will take time and require innovative storytelling and consistent messaging.

AI influencers should ideally not mimic humans too closely. While integrating AI into brand stories is appealing, crossing into the realm of pretending they are real can undermine authenticity.

We might soon see disclaimers like "AI reenactment" on testimonials or reviews presented by AI visuals, similar to the "paid actors" disclaimers in advertisements.

AI influencers might accelerate the decline of consumer trust, exacerbating skepticism towards online endorsements. Genuine content demonstrating a product's effectiveness will become increasingly critical. Expect to see AI influencers modeled after classic mascots but with a digital twist. Imagine Tony the Tiger with real-time social media interaction, blending nostalgia with modern engagement.

While current AI influencer campaigns have seen success, they often appear as novelties rather than sustainable marketing strategies. AI spokespeople can seem artificial and lack transparency, which may not resonate well with consumers long-term. As AI becomes harder to distinguish from humans, people will seek connections. AI avatars that look, sound, and feel like friends can foster a sense of belonging, leading to more AI-driven blogs and content. Despite the rise of AI influencers on social media, most established brands will likely continue to rely on human-based marketing for its authenticity and emotional connection.

These varied perspectives highlight the potential and pitfalls of AI influencers, suggesting a future where they may play a significant role, but with careful and thoughtful implementation.

ON THE VERGE OF REGULATION

Recently, social media platforms have come under increasing scrutiny and are on the verge of more stringent regulation. One major area of concern is the impact of social media usage on the mental health of teenagers. As conversations about this issue intensify, lawmakers and regulatory bodies are responding with new regulations aimed at mitigating potential harm.

There has been a growing body of evidence suggesting that excessive use of social media can negatively affect the mental well-being of young people. Issues such as cyberbullying, social comparison, and exposure to inappropriate content are among the primary concerns. In response, some governments have started to introduce laws that specifically address these problems. For example, new regulations may include age verification measures to ensure that younger users cannot access potentially harmful content, limits on data collection from minors, and requirements for platforms to implement stronger parental controls.

Additionally, there are calls for greater transparency from social media companies about their algorithms and the ways in which they influence user behavior. Policymakers are also advocating for educational programs to teach teens and their parents about safe social media practices and the potential risks associated with excessive use.

These regulatory efforts reflect a broader recognition of the significant role that social media plays in the lives of young people and the need to protect their mental health in an increasingly digital world. As these laws come into effect, they are likely to shape the future landscape of social media, promoting a safer and more mindful approach to its use.

At the center of the new social media war is TikTok, a wildly popular platform owned by ByteDance, a Chinese company. This has sparked an ongoing conflict between the United States government and TikTok, fueled by increasing concerns over cybersecurity and the potential undermining of Western values.

The U.S. government has expressed significant apprehension about the data privacy practices of TikTok. Given that ByteDance is subject to Chinese laws, there are fears that the Chinese government could compel the company to hand over user data, which could then be used for espionage or other malicious activities. This concern is exacerbated by the vast amount of personal information that TikTok collects from its users, including location data, browsing history, and biometric information.

In addition to cybersecurity issues, there are worries about the influence of TikTok on Western values and democratic processes. Critics argue that the platform's content moderation policies could be manipulated to promote Chinese propaganda or to suppress content that is critical of China. There are also broader concerns about the role of social media in spreading misinformation and its impact on political discourse and public opinion.

In response to these concerns, the U.S. government has taken several steps to mitigate the perceived risks associated with TikTok. There have been executive orders aimed at banning the app, although these have faced legal challenges and have yet to be fully implemented. Lawmakers have also proposed legislation that would require stricter oversight of foreign-owned tech companies operating in the United States.

To address these issues, TikTok has made efforts to distance itself from its Chinese parent company. The platform has established data centers outside of China to store user data and has proposed measures to increase transparency and accountability in its operations. Despite these efforts, skepticism remains, and the debate over TikTok's role in the U.S. continues to be a contentious topic.

As the social media landscape evolves, the clash between the U.S. government and TikTok underscores the broader geopolitical tensions between the United States and China. It highlights the need for robust regulatory frameworks to address the complex challenges posed by global technology companies and the importance of safeguarding both national security and democratic values in the digital age.

Regardless of what happens with TikTok, the overarching issues of data privacy, mental health, and other related concerns will always cast a shadow over all social media platforms.

Data privacy remains a critical issue as social media companies collect vast amounts of personal information from their users. This data can be used to enhance user experience through personalized content and advertisements, but it also raises significant privacy concerns. The potential for misuse of this data—whether through breaches, unauthorized access, or even legal but ethically questionable uses—poses a persistent risk. Users are becoming increasingly aware of how their data is handled, demanding more transparency and stricter data protection measures from these platforms.

Mental health is another significant concern, especially with the rise in social media usage among teens and young adults. Numerous studies have highlighted the potential negative impacts of social media on mental health, including increased anxiety, depression, and feelings of loneliness. Issues like cyberbullying, social comparison, and the pressure to present a curated and often unrealistic version of oneself can exacerbate these problems. Social media companies are being called upon to take more responsibility for the well-being of their users, implementing features that promote healthier usage patterns and providing resources for those who may be struggling.

In addition to data privacy and mental health, other issues such as misinformation, digital addiction, and the influence of algorithms also persist. Misinformation can spread rapidly on social media, influencing public opinion and even affecting election outcomes. Digital addiction, driven by the constant notifications and the rewarding nature of social media interactions, can lead to excessive screen time and distract from real-world activities. Algorithms that prioritize engagement can create echo chambers, reinforcing users' existing beliefs and contributing to societal polarization.

As social media continues to evolve, these concerns will remain at the forefront. Platforms must navigate the delicate balance between innovation and responsibility, ensuring that their growth does not come at the expense of user welfare. Regulatory bodies and policymakers are increasingly stepping in to address these challenges, pushing for more comprehensive regulations that protect users while fostering a fair and competitive digital marketplace.

The issues of data privacy, mental health, and other related concerns are not just specific to any single platform like TikTok but are inherent to the nature of social media itself. The ongoing dialogue and actions surrounding these issues are crucial in shaping a more secure, healthy, and ethical digital environment for all users.

WHAT IS SOCIAL MEDIA?

So, what is social media, exactly? Well, it is any mechanism that allows people to share things — media — which can range from text to pictures and videos, it includes comments, likes, ratings, or other qualifiers that people have added, or simply content that people (and not publishers), have created themselves.

Facebook, for example, is not a 'social medium,' but rather a platform by which these media can be socialized, or shared. And in this sense, all media are essentially 'social' — even printed newspapers or magazines — though today's online platforms make this sharing far easier. Our grandparents tore articles out of their media and mailed them to friends. Now, we do that in an instant, and many of us generate our own content to share.

It is the social aspect of social media that is most important to understand. This essentially means people sharing media with one another. The majority of what is shared on social media is User Generated Content, or 'UGC,' but that does not mean businesses cannot get involved.

In fact, this person-to-person sharing is the key to businesses' successful use of social media. Every business wants to build and generate purchase intent among existing and new customers – and, while methods like digital display might be good for getting the word out about your products, recommendations from family, friends and trusted influencers are a great way of driving purchase intent.

Of course, buying display ads or other, more 'traditional' media is also easier to control. After all, if you are relying on social sharing, you need to 'earn' a place in conversations. But understanding social media sharing is the backbone of any social media strategy.

Social media is all but unavoidable these days; just think about how much time you or your friends and relatives spend using it. You are not alone; you are part of a global phenomenon that is transforming how we discover, interpret, and use information. In fact, studies show that the average internet user spends over 2 hours each day on social media. This means that today, social media less an alternative method of communication, and more a primary, if not preferred way to share and consume information.

It is also a particularly mobile experience. People's use of their phones and other mobile devices to access the internet surpassed their usage on desktop computers back in 2016, and monthly use of mobile devices in the US alone is approaching 100 hours each month, which is around 3 hours a day on average.

So, what are they...we...doing on our phones? Chatting and researching, mostly, and being entertained whilst we do it.

Naturally, we are also talking about brands, however this person-to-person sharing that is happening so often via mobile technology is far less with brands, and far more about them, as well as about what people think and do with them. Studies have shown that a whopping 96% of those who discuss brands online do not actually "follow" those brands' owned, online channels.

In terms of how businesses use social media, the early adopters were consumer brands, which is not surprising, and in fact the top 20 brands on Facebook - in terms of followers - are all B2C.

But that is changing, and today the vast majority of businesses that sell only to other businesses have a social presence, too, thanks to the broad usage and changing nature of social media. The reasons B2B and B2C companies use social are obviously as diverse as the businesses themselves.

In addition to the established uses by marketers to communicate about their products or services, customer service is a powerful and growing area. While traditional touchpoints are still popular, over a third of customers prefer to use social media to contact businesses. Interestingly, the dynamic of this contact changes with the medium, too: we all know what it is like sitting on the phone waiting for a customer service representative. Social media users expect responses quickly, if not immediately.

Combine this with the use of social media on mobile platforms, and you can imagine those service issues being experienced, and hopefully resolved, as they happen.

Another use for social media that is on the rise is customer and product research. Lots of brands utilize this approach, such as LEGO, whose online community 'LEGO Ideas' allows fans to submit, vote on and give feedback about designs for new sets. As well as collecting valuable and authentic feedback, it is a way of rewarding loyal customers, and winners get to see their LEGO sets created and sold worldwide.

Social media can enable you to reach more people and, more importantly, reach the right people, as well as doing so quickly and more frequently. General Electric, the industrial giant, uses this aspect of social media to gather insights that are applicable across the entire organization. This approach, called "social intelligence," enables the collection and understanding of what its customers, vendors, partners, and other important stakeholder groups think and expect, and uses those insights to better inform strategic planning and development

In a public-facing bid to improve its environmental credentials, and as part of its long-running 'Ecomagination' strategy, GE partnered with Virgin Airlines to offer prizes for the best insights regarding what it called a 'social airplane.'

The company enlisted a community of over 90,000 people following its @ecomagination Twitter account, and using certain hashtags, organized conversations around key topics such as sustainability and green energy. This approach mobilized a global network to rapidly contribute original ideas such as using solar panels in manufacturing, LED lights on aircraft and even messaging passengers directly when their row is boarding.

Social media caters for a variety of business activities, not just marketing. This is important to remember when you are considering ways it might benefit your business. Think beyond marketing, to the ways your company communicates with its audience — marketers call themselves stakeholders because they have a "stake" in your company's performance — and how peer-to-peer sharing might influence it.

BRANDS ON SOCIAL MEDIA

If we are going to consider social media as something far richer and more nuanced than simply a way to place ads — despite this area of digital marketing being so successful — we should ask ourselves the question "how do brands achieve that exposure?" After all, it is one thing to identify sharing as the vital mechanism that makes social media so interesting and valuable, but how do brands get that sharable content into conversations if they are not buying it outright? Well, there are three core ways it gets done: publishing, curating and thought leadership.

Publishing on social media means creating things — text stories, audio, videos, anything that has information in it, which we can generalize and call "content" — and then sharing it on social platforms, in hopes that people will see value in sharing it with one another. These activities are incredibly diverse and often fascinating, but one quality that they all share is that they are not commercial messages in any traditional sense of the term; the best shareable content published by brands is not about promoting a product or service, but rather - providing content that is entertaining, informative, and ideally useful to people, whilst being relevant to those products and services for which your brand is known.

There are plenty of examples of this, everything from the airline KLM publishing fun facts articles — called "Airplane Mysteries" — which, of course, got people thinking and talking about airline travel... To Elon Musk's Space X, which makes space rockets, publishes video footage of its rocket tests, sometimes including footage of failures and crashes, which contributes to peoples' belief that it is authentic and transparent.

In fact, transparency is an important quality for all communications these days — more than just claiming to be credible and honest, it is how it is proven — and many businesses use social media to achieve this. Coca-Cola is one of many brands that publish content on manufacturing practices and many transport companies publish updates on delays (including explaining them, which travelers tend to appreciate).

You can almost qualify the most 'effective' content published for social media sharing as: that which would not qualify if it were overtly declared and paid for, such as in an advertisement. On social media, people "buy" published content with their interest and willingness to forward it.

The second way businesses participate in social media is by "curating," which means finding and forwarding content created by others, whether related to a brand (which might be one of their own customers) or simply found on the web. This approach has the added benefits of: making more content available to share, trading on the authenticity and credibility of others, and potentially giving interested stakeholders exposure, which they appreciate.

For instance, a resort guide called The Bali Bible used Instagram to give travelers advice, and by encouraging them to post their own recommendations using The Bali Bible hashtag, greatly expanded its own presence in conversations. Slack, a project collaboration software service, curated positive comments from users and shared them with the hashtag "SlackLoveTweets." Remember, a hashtag is simply a designator in front of a term that makes it searchable on certain online platforms. It is also a way to get a brand name into that sharable content.

Finally, businesses create content that is newsworthy, which gets picked up and shared by news organizations as well as individuals. This is most often accomplished by creating content that challenges the status quo, illuminates a difficult topic, is surprising, or otherwise has inherent value. It is often called "thought leadership," which means, simply, that businesses share thoughts that lead to further investigation and exploration.

Elon Musk did this when he hosted events at which he talked about populating the solar system with a network of rocket services. Now, of course, it is pretty unlikely that your company is planning something so audacious... and it is not necessary. What matters is that your thought leadership provides value to people outside of your business, and does not simply rely on what you want to tell them. Consider these two examples: The makers of Oreo cookies chose to take a stand on LGBT rights, and surprised its many millions of Facebook followers with a rainbow-themed cookie picture, which was shared thousands of times. Also, room sharing service AirBnB took a stand on immigration by sharing content with the hashtag WeAccept during the Super Bowl, and generated a huge amount of awareness.

It is important to note that achieving this kind of thought leadership exposure via social media is truly a business strategy, since almost half of CEOs say that they look to this content to decide whether or not to ask for bids from businesses.

One last aspect of how businesses use social media that is worth exploring is the function of "influencers."

Generally, the recommendations that mean the most to people are from family and friends, but in close second place are 'influencers. Influencers are, just like the word suggests, people who have the ability to reach others with compelling information; they are credible experts and individuals, often journalists, who spend the time and effort to share their opinions and insights on social media. Their ability to sway public opinion should not be underestimated: nearly half of consumers say they rely on influencers to help them make decisions, and an overwhelming majority of them trust what influencers say more than what companies say.

The most popular social media platform for influencers to use is Instagram, mainly because simple visuals are great at driving engagement and responses, but every social media platform is worth considering and potentially using. There are even complex digital tools that enable businesses to map and then track the effects of influencers, accurately tracing what gets shared with whom.

Celebrities are a unique category of influencers, as many of them have immense followings on social media platforms. While they can share their heartfelt opinions on things, many of them sell their names and reputations to marketers, which is not much different than the old-fashioned celebrity endorsements of decades past. Today's stars can get exposure for brands that pay for the privilege, but that awareness is nowhere near as meaningful or lasting as when it is shared by influencers who truly believe in what they are sharing.

A common way for businesses to earn that exposure is by giving selected influencers discount coupons that they can share with their followers on social media. Swedish watchmaker Daniel Wellington took this approach and offered a caption for a 15% discount to sit alongside image posts featuring its watches in aesthetic settings that were natural and authentic to the influencers. This campaign helped the watchmaker explode from a start-up to a brand worth $220 million in less than 5 years.

Another way is to give influencers exclusive access to information, like Waymo did on its secretive development of a self-driving car. The idea is to provide influencers with information that will be valuable not only to them, but to the people who rely on them for information.

Working with influencers draws on many of the same principles that drive publishing, curation, and thought leadership. B2C and B2B brands use social media to talk about things that matter to their customers and other stakeholders, and do so in ways that are relevant, useful, and usually not obvious sales messages. Perhaps that is why it is called "content" instead of "ads."

ISSUES & THEMES

Social media is a constantly evolving landscape, so let us briefly explore three major issues that are relevant to your business' use of it. The first issue is privacy.

People are becoming more and more concerned about how their data is collected and used; after all, 'digital' offers businesses ways of identifying and tracking people, and that includes their online names and behavioral information gathered from social media. What can constitute a "good thing" — gaining a better understanding of who your business is talking to or, just as importantly, who is talking to and potentially influencing whom — could cross the line and be viewed as creepy and intrusive if that information is used for suspect purposes... or if people are simply worried that it might be.

You really cannot afford to underestimate this issue. And the issue is destined to become more pressing, as 2017 saw more hacks than the year before, as well as some of history's all-time largest thefts. Every year now, companies experience tens of millions of cyberattacks worldwide, and the increasing use of devices connected to the Internet of Things — such as your home assistant or smart car — will only increase the risks for everyone.

In addition to your business needing to robustly protect the data you collect, this issue requires that you also consider what data you even want to collect in the first place (in other words, is the risk of possessing it greater than your need to use it?). The days of simply aggregating it and choosing what to do with it later are long gone.

Government scrutiny and potential action will also influence your decisions around privacy. Europe's GDPR intends to strengthen consumer data protection, which will have impacts for corporate policy. American Federal agencies are also looking more closely at how businesses gather, store, and use data. No brand can contemplate social media strategies without serious consideration of data security and privacy policies first.

The second issue is metrics, or how you plan to measure the return on your investment in social media activities. We will get to the details in later chapters, but from a big picture perspective, it is important to note that there is really no consensus on how to best measure the effectiveness of social media.

Early on, the metrics were imported from the analog marketing world, so B2C marketers looked to track awareness and survey recall, much the same way they did with print advertising, and then created new ones that were exclusive to social media platforms, such as "engagement" which can be a measure of likes or shares, or both.

One of the problems could be that it is relatively easy to game the system, regardless of what metrics you use. There is a thriving industry of vendors who supply followers — so your business can literally buy fans, so to speak — only those followers can be disinterested, and do little to no sharing, or be bots... so not even real people at all. One estimate of Twitter accounts that were not actually people was nearly 48 million. So, it is no surprise that quantities of followers or likes might not correlate with measurable business results.

It is not that any business is doing something wrong; it is just that social media "fame" is not synonymous with an effective social strategy, and thankfully more companies are coming to realize this fact.

The third issue is quite broad, but perhaps best characterized as the pushback against tech. Everywhere you turn these days, there are claims of "fake news" or concerns around some illicit or illegal use of social media. To be honest, there are even bigger questions being asked about technology's overall role in society:

Facebook has admitted that it may be a negative for democracy, and the late, great physicist Stephen Hawking was not alone in pondering aloud whether technologies like Artificial Intelligence could spell the end of the human race.

Add to this the unease you or I might feel about our privacy, or how technology is changing our lives for the better or worse, and you can see what could be an emerging issue. The leading social media platforms certainly see it. There are reasons behind YouTube beginning to shut down channels that share troubling content, and why Facebook is constantly tinkering with its News Feed to discourage blatant hate speech (as well as blatant commercialism).

So, what is a business to do? Well, in this chapter we have discussed the compelling reasons why businesses might want to use social media, and shared a number of examples of ways to do it. The issues of privacy, metrics, and tech pushback are important for you to consider when you explore the 'why' and 'how.' Social media, like any public activity, does not come without risks. The key to its successful use is found in assessing and implementing those efforts with a keen eye on the potential benefits and drawbacks.

NEW DEVELOPMENTS
AND SOCIAL PLATFORMS

Having discussed the context and themes around social media, let us assume that you are now researching using social media and looking for answers to some big questions: What are the newest developments from social media players? What are the top platforms, who uses them, and how? And, of course - what should you consider in establishing the framework for how you might participate?

First and foremost, it's crucial to remember that your followers on social media are not truly yours; they are users of the platform. This distinction has significant implications for anyone relying heavily on social media for their audience engagement. You face several risks: being deplatformed, canceled, or affected by the platform losing its popularity, which could lead to users migrating to another service. To mitigate these risks and ensure long-term sustainability, it's essential to develop a strategy to capture first-party user data, reducing dependency on social media platforms.

One of the most effective ways to capture first-party data is by building an email list. Encourage your social media followers to subscribe to your newsletter by offering valuable content, exclusive updates, or incentives like discounts and freebies. Email marketing allows direct communication with your audience, ensuring you maintain contact even if social media platforms change their algorithms or policies.

Having your own website or blog serves as a central hub for your content and brand. By driving traffic from your social media profiles to your website, you can engage users more deeply and collect their data through sign-ups, surveys, and interactions. This platform independence means you retain control over your audience relationship regardless of social media trends.

Provide exclusive content or membership options that require users to register on your site. This strategy not only captures user data but also builds a more committed and engaged audience. Platforms like Patreon or your own membership site can be effective for this purpose, offering exclusive access to content, events, or products.

Implementing a Customer Relationship Management (CRM) system can help manage and analyze your interactions with followers, turning them into meaningful data. CRM systems enable you to track user behavior, preferences, and engagement patterns, helping tailor your content and marketing strategies more effectively.

Webinars and live events are excellent for gathering first-party data. Require registration to participate, capturing emails and other relevant information. These events also allow for deeper interaction with your audience, fostering a stronger sense of community and loyalty.

Organize contests and giveaways that require participants to provide their email addresses or other contact information. This not only captures data but also increases engagement and can help expand your reach as participants share the event with their networks.

While diversifying your presence across multiple social media platforms can reduce risk, it's also a way to capture more user data. Encourage your followers to engage with you on various platforms, increasing your touchpoints and the likelihood of maintaining contact if one platform declines.

And now, let's talk about social media itself.

NEW DEVELOPMENTS

People have enjoyed stories since time began, and so, they are - and probably always will be - an effective and reliable way of sharing content.

One of the most popular new innovations on this front comes from Instagram, which enables users to post images and videos over a 24-hour period - after which they disappear.

It is actually called 'Stories,' and Facebook has since followed in Instagram's footsteps, providing its users with a similar feature. Many social platforms also boast video sharing capabilities that let users, both businesses and individuals alike, create channels through which they can share their content - whether that is carefully curating posts or live-streaming an event as it is unfolding.

The power of storytelling has not gone unnoticed by Twitter either. After initially limiting users to 140 characters per post, it has since increased the maximum to 280 characters - in a bid to increase engagement across the platform.

This being said, many of the stories being told on social media remain out of reach for most brands, at least directly. Reddit is an ever-popular platform whose users stubbornly reject even the slightest hint of commercialism; and their Reditquette rules reflect that.

More so than many other platforms, this community forum is a domain where individuals - not corporations - rule the roost, sharing things that are important to them. But, in some circumstances, brands have overcome these restrictions, usually by arranging for an individual to contribute to conversations without making a sales pitch.

Participation gets even harder for brands when you consider that social sharing is not limited to the platforms we have just discussed - a lot of sharing actually happens through private messaging apps such as Apple's iMessage, Google's Hangouts, and even the ubiquitous WhatsApp. Known as 'dark social,' these activities cannot be measured through web analytics.

Social media can be a great place to make your stories heard, even as a brand, but remember: in these spaces, people want to talk to one another, and not necessarily to a business. You should also bear this in mind when looking towards new social sharing opportunities...

One intriguing development is the emergence of Augmented Reality, or "AR" technology which superimposes digital information over the world around us - achieving a seamless integration of the two.

So, think about all of the content you look down to your phone to consume - weather, maps, restaurant reviews, even product descriptions. Now imagine that appearing in front of you instead, so you experience it live and as a part of the real world around you.

For Instance, Snapchat offers a service that lets users create DIY augmented reality 'World Lenses.' 'Lens Studio,' a desktop app, allows anyone to create a lens, submit it for publication, and then share it using a scannable code.

Naturally, Snapchat has developed opportunities for advertisers too; rolling out 'Sponsored Lenses' that let companies insert their branding and products into a user's experience, and incorporate "Buy," "Watch" or "Install" buttons. This way, when users apply these lenses, they are engaging with the brand and broadcasting its commercial offers at the same time. One of the first brands to take this opportunity was Bud Light with its virtual beer vendor passing out bottles... And research shows that the average sponsored lens contributes to significant gains in both ad awareness and brand awareness.

The rolling out of AR kits by Apple, Google and others could prove to be a gamechanger, allowing the creation of branded AR apps. In IKEA's case, its app allows users to virtually place different furniture around their home to see what it would look like, helping them to make purchase decisions without even needing to visit a store.

As tech companies grace the AR stage with offerings of their own, the space is sure to become complex and fragmented - especially in terms of strategy - but the potential opportunities for brands are fascinating.

There are many ways social media platforms can facilitate storytelling right now, some intriguing tech on the horizon, and certain sharing platforms that remain stubbornly resistant to, or even out of reach to businesses.

To really succeed on social media, you will need to base your efforts on the value you can bring to real conversations and connections. Forcing your brand front and center probably won't give you the results you're looking for, and as advertising and other paid placement opportunities multiply, remember: inspiring and shareable content is the true driver of social media strategy...and success.

Social Platforms

There are many platforms occupying the social media space, and each has its own mechanisms for posting and sharing content, and each attracts somewhat different users... who visit for somewhat different reasons.

This being said, there is a good deal of convergence going on, with platforms pursuing similar features in order to adapt to new conditions, needs and expectations.

So, let us take a look at them one by one and get a good picture of how they might be useful to your business.

Facebook is the long-reigning champion of social media, and almost a third of the total population of the planet uses it. According to one study, over 9 out of 10 businesses use Facebook, and it is no wonder! It gives them access to a wide audience, advanced measurement capabilities for understanding those users and a robust set of tools for engaging with them.

On Facebook, you can make a page for your company, which can act as a 'home' for your business: an effective hub for company information, branded content, and your brand community. What is more important, though, is what you promote or launch from your page. At its heart, Facebook is all about connecting with users, and creating content that they will want to share and interact with.

As a feature that gives users the opportunity to broadcast video in real time, Facebook Live connects users to events as they are happening, making them feel like they are part of the action. It can be used to inform and attract audiences, through sneak peaks or Q&As, or for purely entertainment purposes, like Buzzfeed's live stream of an exploding watermelon which received more than 11 million views.

Brands have traditionally relied on driving engagement on Facebook through 'organic content' which users find and share in their newsfeeds. Nowadays though, thanks to changes to Facebook's algorithm, this engagement is increasingly being generated by paid ads.

'Facebook Watch,' for example, a video-on-demand service launched by the company in late 2017, lets brands buy ad breaks, sponsor content, or even create their own branded shows.

Facebook's additional ownership of Instagram and WhatsApp means that it holds a formidable amount of data on its users.

With this in mind, it is also a great place to serve users 'dynamic ads' - content that has been specifically targeted towards, and tailored to users based on who they are and how they behave online.

Facebook's users tend to be a little older than other platforms, but its user base is so broad it defies easy characterization. It can be a great place to show the human side of your brand, which does not always come across on a corporate website. Be sure to create varied, entertaining, and relevant content that your followers will want to share!

Acting primarily as a photo sharing application and service, Instagram could be considered the most popular social platform with Millennials, with over half of those in the US using it. Now owned by Facebook, it offers various ways for advertisers to buy exposure across the two platforms, all the while, retaining the social sharing values responsible for its initial success.

Instagram allows companies to create branded accounts. They do not offer the breadth of functionality provided by those on Facebook, but brands like Starbucks are still using Instagram to great effect.

The coffee giant posts both its own content, and user generated content from fans, to an audience of more than 17 million followers. For many years now, Starbucks has spearheaded its RedCupContest campaign on the platform, revealing the latest iteration of its iconic Christmas coffee cup and encouraging users to post their own pictures too.

We have already mentioned Instagram Stories, montages of photos or videos that can be shared amongst followers for 24 hours. Well, they are hugely popular, with more than 400 million daily active users in 2018.

It should come as no surprise that Instagram now offers an additional service called 'Stories Highlights,' which allows users to archive this content into albums and keep them on their account page indefinitely.

Lots of brands make great use of Stories, especially due to the 'stickers' that can be used within them. These can be hashtags or mentions, which put your company name prominently within content that features your brand, while Location Stickers let users tag images and video clips to specific places.

Stickers can be a great way for keeping your brand on top - if a user searches for your brand, store location or a trending hashtag, they can engage with relevant content - whether that is images and videos that you have created, or User Generated Content that you have been tagged in.

Instagram can be seen as more fast-paced, short-term, and 'social' than platforms that host longer-form videos or text. That said, it was actually Snapchat that first pioneered this kind of ephemeral social media content — a platform that allows users to send and receive messages with a short lifespan, disappearing a matter of seconds after being opened. Interestingly, Snapchat calls itself "a camera company," which tells you that it sees itself less as a screen for consuming visual content, and more as a tool for creating it.

Above anything else, Snapchat prioritizes its individual users. In fact, it actually places their content ahead of promoted content from brands or paid influencers – so it is up to businesses to make sure their content is of a high enough quality so that users will actually want to share it.

Just like on Instagram, Snapchat allows users to create Stories - the snippets of visual content that exist for only a day. Brands can produce this content, or encourage their followers to do so, and then layer different tools - like Sponsored Filters and Lenses, and Snapcodes - on top for marketing purposes.

Filters let brands create a graphic that 'Snapchatters' can superimpose on their own content, and thereby promote the brand too. These can be used to create proactive campaigns, like the non-profit organization RED did on World AIDS Day, making a donation for every one of the 14 million Snapchatters who sent a message using one of its filters.

Sponsored Lenses are similar to filters, but even more interactive. Gatorade, for instance, created a Sponsored Lens that allowed users to add animation to their selfies, making them look as if they were getting drenched just like coaches do at the end of an American football game - it received 165 million views. In addition, you might choose to develop Snapcodes, which are like QR codes, and when scanned, they unlock new content for users to explore.

Snapchat is seen as a playful Instagram which is pursuing a somewhat different, more user-centric goal. This might make it a little more difficult for marketers to exploit with paid ads, but it could be said that its focus on user content makes its sharing and engagement more valuable. Well, that is the bet Snapchat are making anyway.

Staying on a visual theme, [4] Pinterest is a virtual scrapbook that allows individuals and brands to collect content from the web and "pin" it to a personally curated board, which is then searchable by other users.

Shared interests like food, fashion and DIY have fueled Pinterest's popularity and made it a global success.

Pinterest is still primarily the domain of individual users, but you will also find B2C brands are getting involved, too. For businesses and entrepreneurs, such collections of pins can amount to virtual storefronts from which they can also sell their wares. Retailer, Target has over 100 million pins for its posts, most of which are products, and links that take visitors to its store. Brands can also promote relevant content for their followers, by bringing together content published on other sites, or simply tagging other articles.

But it is not just about B2C. Several B2B businesses such as General Electric and NASA are using Pinterest as a way of connecting with their customers and exploring a more 'playful' side of the company.

Moving away from the more strictly 'social' sharing platforms, there are a number of key players that offer interesting opportunities for brands - if they are approached correctly...

Founded back in 2002 and owned by Microsoft, LinkedIn is a social media platform for professionals and is commonly used as a recruitment and networking tool.

Like other social sites, you can create a page for your company, and with the help of its Pages offering - revamped late in 2018 - you can present information about your business, share materials, and create, track, and engage in conversations that are relevant to you.

This should continue to allow LinkedIn to serve as a powerful content publishing platform in its own right. Whilst maintaining a list of featured thought leaders called 'Linkedin Influencers,' it allows any person or brand to post articles and build an audience.

'Thought leadership' is prevalent on the platform, but it is generally agreed that compared to other social networks, LinkedIn is not the best place to be particularly controversial. This leads many brands to post regurgitated marketing content more often than creating original content for the platform, but that is not necessarily the way to unlock LinkedIn's higher potential...

LinkedIn offers programmatic ad opportunities for brands to match their marketing content to a specified audience. Take SAS, for example, a software company that was looking to generate leads by driving downloads of its whitepaper. By using LinkedIn's targeted display ad opportunities, it was able to reach the exact intended audience: HR professionals in companies with 1000 or more employees.

LinkedIn also provides an advanced messaging service called Sponsored InMail, which lets users send content to other LinkedIn members to which they are not connected. You can target these members by selecting filters such as location, industry, and job title.

Sponsored InMail has taken measures to improve the likelihood that your content is seen, by only delivering messages when their recipients are active on the platform, and imposing frequency caps to limit the number of times that a single member can receive messages over a set period of time.

Twitter is another big platform, and there are a variety of ways to use it; in fact, it is helpful to think of it as both a platform for social interaction and, based on the success of its tagging or 'hashtag' functionality, a searchable database for information. For this reason, it is really worth considering if, and how, you want to place your business there.

Twitter users find content by "following" other people and businesses, receiving updates when posts appear. Most companies use Twitter to share updates on their business activities, and often it is the first place for announcements, just as it is often the first place that breaking news can be found. This functionality is useful to every type of business, even B2B.

Twitter is a great publicity tool but it can also be used for customer service, where brands can engage with customers and respond to enquiries and grievances visibly and in real-time.

It is also seen as a suitable platform for thought leadership, as many CEOs use it to communicate more personal ideas that are not necessarily company announcements, but are still relevant to their industry. Twitter is a platform that gives companies numerous ways to engage in social conversations, and its users span nearly all age groups and demographics.

All of the social platforms we have covered so far have a wide range of content sharing or hosting capabilities, but there are others which owe their continuing success to video alone...

YouTube is the original and still most widely used video sharing platform. It is making significant moves to monetize its services by offering paid, produced TV channels, the most popular of which are game-based and primarily oriented towards young audiences. But, from early on it tapped into people's interest in creating and viewing video, and businesses use it in a variety of ways...

Like other social platforms, YouTube lets companies create branded channels on which they can house videos and collect followers. Toymaker LEGO's page, for example, hosts over 20 thousand videos and now boasts more than 7.3 million subscribers. YouTube can be used for purely commercial purposes, or to raise awareness on wider issues. 'Circles,' a campaign by Levi's jeans, promoted multicultural tolerance and celebrated unity through music, dance, and of course, its products, receiving over 25 million views on YouTube alone.

Product reviews, instructions for use, and repair tips are a thriving area for content. These can be created by businesses, like car-maker Ford who received almost 20 million views for its "Do not Drive Distracted" video, or by influencer accounts like 'DOPE or NOPE', which has over 6 million subscribers tuning in to its "unboxing" videos of new and interesting products. A twist on this approach is providing broader instructional, educational videos, like the do-it-yourself segments produced by Home Depot. It is also worth noting that YouTube is often the go-to channel for customers looking to do research - in fact, it is the world's 2nd largest search engine... after Google.

Whilst YouTube is by far the largest online video platform globally, it' s not the only one. Vimeo is much smaller and has a different structure for brand participation and pricing, but many businesses find it worthwhile to maintain a presence here too.

With new social platforms coming online all the time, the challenge (and the opportunity!) is to consider which ones are best suited to your business purposes. You could produce something to put on any of them; but choosing which ones, and why, remains the most important social media strategy you can embrace.

Your social presence

Having looked at the different platforms, let us explore the key points, and potential trade-offs, your social media strategy might face.

You will need to find the balance between declaring and sharing. Remember, content that is exclusively attached to a brand, or feels heavily branded, is rarely the most popular. This could be a difficult trade-off if you are looking at spending a limited budget on your marketing communications overall, and senior managers who aren't social media users themselves may legitimately ask "why do it?"

Then, there is the balancing of targeting and attracting. Social media platforms are tools for digital marketing, and provide a variety of ways to identify and target users, often funneling them to other sites and potential data capture.

Some of the most interesting business uses of social media throw these principles to the wind, however, in the hope of attracting new views from people that may not have emerged from any targeting activity. For example, The Financial Times newspaper chose to publish intriguing charts on Instagram without referrals back to its site; it simply wanted to attract users. With its account now being followed by 1.4 million users, we can safely say it succeeded.

In order to really get the most from your social media presence, there are some key considerations you will need to take into account - starting with your brand voice.

Let us be honest, most companies talk in a voice that is oddly impersonal, if not quite sterile. There is a tendency to use the corporate or royal "we" to announce things, and stuff marketing brochures with descriptive sentences. Press releases are often populated with buzzwords and big claims, but this would most likely fail if the same approach were used on social platforms.

The crux of social media is person-to-person communications. It is not enough for your content to be formatted correctly to each platform's specifications; it also has to be content that will matter to your users, and spoken in a voice that is personal, real, and human.

Take some time to observe how other businesses communicate on social platforms, especially those you compete with or admire. How could this inspire your own innovative social interactions? Whatever voice your brand ends up adopting, make sure it is consistent once you start using it, otherwise, you risk being viewed as inauthentic.

Along with your brand voice, you also need a good understanding of the resources it will take to pull off the social media endeavors you have in mind. Communicating on social media, like any other communications platform, requires strategy, talent to develop content, and technical resources. It also has some unique requirements. You will need staff to manage the conversations you have opened up and involved yourself in, and approval processes that are faster and more flexible than those used for other company decisions.

You need to map these requirements before you post your first piece of content anywhere. Where will new posts come from, and what will be the rules that guide their creation? Who is ultimately responsible for it?

You might have your brand's voice and resources all figured out, but you also need to be prepared for the potential pushback your social media content could receive. What if your content prompts a genuinely unintended consequence? Are you prepared for a significant number of people to dislike what you have said?

And, are you prepared to not just address these outcomes, but also endure them? Some of the worst crises on social media are not coverage of disasters or product failures, but simply negative reactions to well-intentioned content.

Finally, perhaps the most important consideration you will have to regularly assess when using social media is this: Would your audience care about your content even if you had not paid to push it in front of them? At the end of the day, social media platforms are not really advertising channels. Instead, they are places where users interact with each other, about topics they are interested in, and in a way that is authentic and relevant to them. Your success with social media depends on you recognizing and respecting this fact.

Innovations in social media are many, and the platforms diverse are, but by now we have established the qualities and considerations of a successful strategy. The only thing left to do is to create one.

○ · ◉ · ○

SOCIAL MEDIA STRATEGY

I t is time to think about how to create your social media strategy. We have already looked at what is possible, and you know what your options are, too. The only thing you need now is a strategy to exploit those opportunities.

Importantly - your social media strategy should mirror strategies that your business uses for other activities, not just limited to marketing. Any good strategy has three components: goals, or what you want to accomplish; metrics, or how you will measure that accomplishment, and tools, or the means by which you will achieve your goals.

SETTING GOALS

When you are thinking about setting goals, the first component is to articulate a clear business purpose, which could be anything from increasing sales to... reducing production costs for a certain component. There are at least six potential purposes for any social media strategy; they are not mutually exclusive, but it helps to prioritize them, as it is your business purpose that informs what you will want to communicate, on what platforms, and how often.

When setting social media goals based on your wider business goals, ask yourself what they are, and in what order, from this list:

First, there's brand awareness. Do you want people to recognize your brand more easily or often, or attach some emotion to it? This is what Red Bull did in hopes of boosting awareness of its "Summer Edition" energy drink with yellow filters and images & videos of summer days on Instagram and Pinterest.

Second, maybe it is customer acquisition? Do you want to collect more new business leads? The Girl Scouts wanted to sell more cookies, so focused on driving downloads of their Cookie Finder app via a Twitter campaign.

Third, are you trying to build customer loyalty? When customers of California's Pieology Pizzeria posted an image of one of their pizzas, they were rewarded with a coupon for free cinnamon sticks.

Fourth, what about customer service? Do you want to use social media to resolve problems, like the way Hyatt hotel customers get issues resolved while waiting for a room... not to mention once they are in them?

Fifth, you might want to focus on aggressively selling stuff. Is it possible to prompt sales via social media? Complicated purchases, especially those in B2B settings, probably are not likely candidates - but Nordstrom and other retailers rely on influencers to drive customer traffic to their sites, and finally...

Sixth, do you want to recruit talent? You can look further than LinkedIn job listings alone: for instance, GE's #BalanceTheEquation social media campaign, which targeted women in science and engineering roles in a drive to boost and diversify their workforce, hit nearly a million views on YouTube.

Of course, you can have more than one goal, but they need to be prioritized and ideally the fewer, the better - it is hard to enough to accomplish one thing let alone a few.

The second criteria for effective goal-setting is risk mitigation.

Using social media has its own rules, and much of your efforts will be delivered and judged in real-time, so you need to clearly identify and prepare for them...

First, you need to assess risks and benefits — There is no standard model for doing it, but you need a process to be very vigilant of the potential upsides... and potential downsides... of your social strategy. It is not comforting that most of the worst social "fails" are a result of companies failing to see potential problems that are only too obvious when they actually occur. You might want to consider researching notable social fails and ranking them by how damaging similar fails might be to your company. Consider assigning actual values to each, both in terms of monetary effect and percentage likelihood of happening. Your ultimate enemy is surprise, even if you're utterly successful in your results.

Second, you need to create a clear development process for the content of your social campaigns, as well as the business and legal reviews required for approval. This is particularly important if you have an external agency creating your campaigns. One trick you can use is to use your risk assessment phase as the basis for creating the development team.

It is not enough if the marketing department has decided some creative or specific language is acceptable — and then does a great job of selling their ideas internally — because if other stakeholders within your organization use different criteria for review, or are uninvolved until the last steps before going live, you are just asking for trouble. The more it resembles the development processes you use for other activities, the better it will be!

Perhaps most importantly, be ready to respond to crises — You need to be prepared when there's negative pushback to your campaign, which first means having the analysis and tracking tools in place to recognize audience reaction as early as possible. Crises are horrible times to figure out how to do things so you not only need a plan to respond, but a team informed and equipped to do the responding.

Give people exact responsibilities. Figure out who has to talk to whom, and where the approvals are found. Many companies have that one executive that needs to weigh in on issues if they reach a certain level; is that person clearly identified in the response plan? And, finally, have you practiced it? All other emergency responders' practice, and you really should, too.

Next, it is time to think about the guidelines for your strategy for content development. As with the rest of your preparation, you need to make these decisions before you task someone or some team, inside or outside of your organization, to begin with their efforts.

There are three broad content criteria to consider. First, it is that issue of 'corporate voice,' since you cannot decide how you are going to communicate on social media until you have decided what business goals you are trying to accomplish, and what risks you might face in trying to reach them...

How personal are you willing to make your content? The more authentic it is, the better. But it does not have to be 'perfect': there is no way that every social post will embody every fact or attribute of your brand. And do not be afraid to be bold: taking a stand on something might not thrill everyone, but your content will compete with literally an endless reservoir of other content, so your willingness to assert a strong point or contradictory position will affect the value of your effort.

You should create actual content (or at the very least find examples) in this phase of your planning, and circulate it to your development team and other internal stakeholders. Everyone will have a different opinion on what you are proposing, and of what "risk" or "bold" actually means.

Additionally, which formats are you willing to use? It is all too common for businesses' use of social media to center around the repurposing of marketing images; beauty shots of products, machines, or that ever-present shot of the happy-faced executives sitting around a conference table making decisions together. Most of these images fall flat on social media because they are not authentic, and they have no personality or attitude.

So, which images will you use, and where will they come from? And who will approve them? Again, you should create these images and make sure everyone approves of what you plan to do. You should always be asking yourself "why" would this picture matter to anyone, and why are we willing to share it?

Finally, you should ask yourself if your voice will be credible on multiple platforms. You do not just want to provide people with a variety of ways to find and share your content, but also to raise your brand's position in search results, which usually means posting on a number of platforms. And it is very rare that can you use identical content on all of them, since their formats and audiences differ so much.

METRICS AND MEASUREMENT

Once you have your goals, risks, and 'voice' in place, you need to think about what measure you will use to track your performance. Put simply, if you cannot measure something, it does not exist, at least not in a business setting. There will always be qualitative outcomes from your efforts — comments, good or bad, that get shared in the organization, but you need to create the criteria by which you will measure the business outcomes of your work.

There are an almost endless array of vendors and tools for doing this. But before you give them a project remit, you need to establish the metrics that matter most to you. Tell them about your business goals, not just your goals for social media activities...

There are two routes you can take to approach this challenge; the first is to use traditional PR-like metrics, many of which are focused exclusively on your brand's performance on specific social platforms.

There are five basic categories you can consider tracking - they are not mutually exclusive but, again, you should prioritize them:

Tracking likes and shares is probably the simplest and most obvious way to measure social performance, as viewers are literally registering their reaction (and subsequent actions...) on the platform. So, you can set a benchmark you hope to reach, or a percentage improvement in numbers over time. You can also analyze your competitors' numbers and set out to better compete with them, or even benchmark your likes and shares against other, non-competitive brands as appropriate.

You might want to track followers - collecting names, in general, is a key component of gathering new potential customers, and social metrics can focus on things like follower growth, whether or not your campaigns have any momentum, and even if there are differences between content that engages infrequent followers versus more constant ones.

'Substance' is also important - maybe it is important to your business that you get certain words or ideas into conversations. You can measure your success doing it by tracking hashtag use (remember: a lot of the best campaigns use hashtags for this very reason), shares of a URL, or even the appearance of certain words.

You might want to measure influencer engagement. You can sharply limit and define the people, or influencers, you want to reach - giving direction on their use of hashtags or referrals, or even distribution of your content (like discount coupons.) This way, you can be sure that their activity aligns with your specified measure of success.

And finally, there's awareness. This is the broadest metric of social performance — assessing how many people overall may have seen your shares — but if you correlate it with sales or some other tangible behavior in the real world (like job applications, for instance), it can have real value. The second group of measures are more related to recognized ad-like metrics, so they are focused on sales-related behaviors, such as:

Clicks. Maybe you want numbers that are concrete proof that your social content delivered value in terms of visitors doing things (liking, sharing, buying and so on). The standard measure for online ad rates has been just those aggregate clicks over the money you spent to achieve them.

Conversions. If your business purpose is to sell things, you can measure how many new customers were gained through your social media presence. This can be done through comparing their emails or other digital identifiers with your list of existing customers.

Share of wallet. You can compare current purchases to past ones, and decide whether or not you are getting more business from your customers.

Loyalty. There are a whole host of metrics for measuring customer loyalty, from amount and frequency of purchases, to engagement with content marketing campaigns, or a combination of factors. You can measure whether or not your social efforts impact these metrics.

And of course, ROI. This is the ultimate ad and marketing-related measure: Did your spend on social media correlate with increased sales, whether gained in the digital or physical world.

It is worth stressing that whereas these ad-related metrics are all valid, they do not get at the social sharing nature of social media. The PR-related measures speak more to the nature of social media. The key here is to establish some specific metrics that are based on your business purpose, and the risk and voice decisions that follow. Once you have made these decisions, you are ready to ask a qualified expert or vendor to provide you with a recommendation on implementation

Achieving your goals

Once you have found the right vendor or agency partner, their recommendation will likely come in the form of a platform selection (or more likely - combination of platforms), and this recommendation will inform the development of your creative and content. Your social effort will likely be based on three communications 'pillars,' using each to varying degrees, depending on the criteria you set out in choosing from the options that we have explored...

One of the pillars will be content that is intended to be directly posted to social platforms. We have covered the basic types of such campaigns, but a few examples at this stage might inspire you.

First off, you could create genuinely entertaining content, which is what many B2C brands do, like the Baby Dragon video ad that Doritos created to promote a spicy 'Heat Wave' addition to their range.

You could create a customer service campaign, like the one car rental brand Hertz did with the business purpose of reducing response time to complaints. They actually managed to improve first response times by 89%!

You can create content intended to challenge and engage influencers, like many brands do by giving a growing base of influencers exclusive access and rewards. Or, you could embrace a cause and take your supportive content directly to social platforms, like CocaCola did to raise money for the World Wildlife Fund.

Another pillar will be mainstream media platforms, which can not only reach your target audiences (yes, people still read magazines), but also generate sharing via social media. There are a number of ways to use mainstream platforms. For instance, many well-known media outlets, from Mashable to the Harvard Business Review, accept contributed articles. It is worth bearing in mind that - as much as publishing or contributing on this kind of platform can give you extra credibility - it also demands a very high quality of content to fit amongst other contributions, otherwise you will stand out for the wrong reason.

Another way is to create an event in the real world and invite media — both traditional and online — to cover it, the way Tesla's announcement of its Model 3 car generated content that was subsequently shared across many social platforms. Dunkin' Donuts did something similar, hosting a first-ever tour of its test kitchen, though they actually hosted it live on Facebook.

The final pillar of your social plan will likely include owned platforms, such as your own website. Employees can also feature in this portion of your plan; though you do not 'own' them, they are a talent pool with a predisposition to support the brand they work for, so companies like Adobe feature content about them both as a recruiting tool, but also to celebrate them.

Social media is here to stay, in large part because it draws on the same qualities that have moved us to share information and content — to tell stories — since the dawn of time. There are numerous reasons to use it, and ways to measure its effectiveness, but the technology platforms that enable us to deliver media socially are only 'as good' as our intentions and ability to create authentic, relevant content to share. What matters is not what you want to tell people… as much as what you legitimately think they may value, and therefore want to share with one another.

Your next step is to experiment. Set an achievable, simple goal, and roll your sleeves up and get stuck in. Engage with your internal and external stakeholders. The cost of entry is relatively low, compared to other activities. Engage with a services provider on a discrete, focused test, and work through your process and content.

○ · ● · ○

PART II
SOCIAL SELLING

SOCIAL SELLING

D igital has impacted pretty much every aspect of business, and both buyers and sellers are feeling the effect - it is changing the way we work, shop, interact and communicate.

Consider social selling not only as a B2B strategy but also as a personal branding opportunity to grow your professional career. Leveraging social selling for personal branding can significantly enhance your professional presence and open new career opportunities. Developing your profile and presence on social networks like LinkedIn is crucial to this process.

Whatever industry or market you work in, you will likely have noticed changes in both your clients' expectations and the ways you have to meet those expectations. It is estimated that nowadays, 67% of the buyer's journey is done digitally, and they now have access to far more information than ever before.

Where previously, the seller drove the conversation, the balance of power has shifted, with a growing number of digitally savvy and informed buyers who now choose when to involve a salesperson in their purchase.

The rise of social media, in particular, has brought with it a whole host of new opportunities. With 75% of B2B buyers saying they use social media in their purchasing decisions, many salespeople are incorporating a long-term social selling strategy into their way of working, in the hopes of fostering more than just sales...

In this section, we will explore what social selling is, why it is come about and what it could mean for you and your business.

WHAT IS SOCIAL SELLING?

Selling and marketing products or services has always been about identifying who your next customer is and where they will be - and putting yourself in front of them. Traditionally, this has been about quite literally being there - think door-to-door selling, cold calling a potential prospect or staffing a stand at an industry event.

Modernizing your sales approach is not about removing these from the equation entirely; instead, it is about recognizing the changes in buyer behavior and understanding that digital tools mean that you now have an even greater opportunity to deliver the right message in the right place at the right time.

The growth of the internet has led to more targeted communications, meaning salespeople can seek out relevant and useful connections, which in turn can lead to new business relationships. Enter: social selling.

In broad terms, social selling is the act of harnessing social networks for business gains. On a day-to-day basis, this will involve liking and commenting on posts, as well as sharing and even creating your own content - playing an active role in the conversations you come across.

Much like traditional networking events, people commonly join social networks to meet like-minded people with shared interests and experiences, to learn from that group, to seek out ideas, opinions, and recommendations, and to share their own knowledge and contribute to the community.

The name 'social selling' can be a bit misleading as most of the time, you will not be actively selling. Although the context is work, people are not there to buy or be sold to, and the temptation to use these networks as a selling platform could quickly lose you those all-important followers. That is why it is often more useful to think of these activities not as social selling, but as social engaging. It is a chance to interact with potential clients and people within your industry, to build relationships over time and even a chance to be seen as an authority.

Once you have built up a reputation, you can then use your connections to get your message to an even wider network, and hopefully make your brand the first one that a buyer in need thinks of.

There are a number of social networking platforms that you might use for social selling, and we will go into these in more detail in our next chapter. For now, though, we will be focusing on LinkedIn.

With 303 million monthly active users, LinkedIn is one of the most popular platforms for professionals worldwide. This means it is also where your connections are most likely to be active.

You may be asking at this point - is not this just social media marketing?

In a word, no, although they are linked. Social media marketing is classified as activities designed to help build brand awareness and engagement without focusing directly on revenue. Social selling, on the other hand, is used to help generate leads and sales outcomes, through building relationships with connections.

If you are embarking on a social selling journey, either as an individual, a team, or a business, you should also engage with any social media marketing activity that your business is running. At the very least, these should be great examples of content that you can share from your own profile, whilst liking or commenting on them could cause posts to appear in the feeds of your followers.

Sales and marketing teams should be working towards the same goals - marketing can help to draw in relevant people, whilst social selling activity could use the established relationship to take buyers further along the sales cycle and bring them closer to a point of purchase.

THE COMMERCIAL VALUE

Whether you are a salesperson yourself, or just have a particularly client-facing role, the end goal is always the same - you want to make a sale. Without a focus on immediate sales, however, social selling needs to be seen as a long-term investment. As with any strategy, businesses want to know that there's commercial value in it. And actually, this new approach can have a real impact on the sales process, both for buyers and sellers.

To see this in action, we will need to take a closer look at the buyer's journey.

Traditionally, the buyer's journey started with a salesperson picking up the phone and telling a buyer about their new product, why it is so good and why they should buy it. Whilst cold calling has always had fairly limited success, there was a time when it was the only way a buyer could learn about your product or service.

Nowadays, buyers carry out a lot of initial research themselves. By the time, a buyer even contacts a salesperson, up to 90% of the selling process could be over and done with. But that does not mean you are only involved in the final stages - you need to be present at every stage of the buyer's journey.

Your buyers will likely start in the awareness phase, where they become aware of a problem or a need.

As they move through the consideration phase - looking at potential solutions for that need, they might become aware of you and your business. Social media is a common place for people to research and ask questions, so that is where you need to be providing answers. It is not about hitting them with a hard sales message in these early stages - they want to be informed, so you need to reach them with information that helps shape their impression of your product or service. By actively engaging with connections, you will also draw in a wider net of people who might not otherwise hear about you.

When your buyers do reach the decision stage, they should already know about you and your offering, so you can focus on closing the deal. Your social selling activity is what helps get buyers to the point of purchase, and your activity needs to complement their journey along the way.

It is important to set expectations when it comes to social selling. Depending on your market and industry, you might find you can generate leads very quickly, but some will require more time and effort. Your typical sales cycle will also be a factor – many of us would expect to nurture a prospect for weeks or months to gain a lead, and the same applies here.

Social selling will undoubtedly help you grow your sales pipeline, but it can provide even wider commercial benefits for you and your business.

Harnessing social media platforms can help salespeople to be more efficient, whilst also alleviating some of the common pain-points of traditional sales. In fact, 39% of B2B professionals said that using social selling tools reduced the amount of time they needed to spend researching accounts and key contacts for potential leads.

As well as helping sales teams to become more efficient, social selling is also very effective at helping salespeople to build relationships that will pay dividends down the line. We all know that relationships are at the core of successful sales, and this is no different just because those conversations have moved online. Now, rather than sticking rigidly to a sales script, you can engage in relevant conversations.

By building relationships and increasing your engagement with your buyers online, you will also increase measures such as LinkedIn's own metric, the

Social Selling Index, or SSI, which considers how you have established your professional brand, how you find the right people, how you engage with insights and how you build relationships. You can benchmark yourself against other members of your team, and even the wider industry to see how you measure up on your social selling abilities. LinkedIn claims that those with a higher score create 45% more opportunities.

Regular, quality social media activity will also help improve your employer's overall brand positioning in the market. Your profile and reach could help you to become an ambassador for the brand, leading to greater traffic to the website, more direct enquiries, and more brand-related searches on Google.

One of the key advantages to the digital world is the amount of data businesses have access to. By spending time crafting new connections and building relationships with followers, you are also gathering huge quantities of data. The ways your connections engage and the content they engage with can provide you with rich insights on who your buyers are and what they need, helping you to be more relevant and valuable. Even a glance at a company's LinkedIn Insights page can show you how many employees have accounts on the platform, breaking down the headcount by function, region, and seniority level.

You will also find that social media data has a longer shelf-life than traditional business data - if a connection changes industry or employer, their old email address and phone number may no longer work, but you can always find them in your LinkedIn network.

One company that uses data to its advantage is Sprinklr - a global social media and customer experience management platform, whose team relied on traditional sales tactics, including cold calls and emails. But as the market matured, Sprinklr realized it needed to evolve and connect with decision-makers in more meaningful ways.

Using LinkedIn's Sales Navigator tool, the team mapped out their key accounts and used this information to find potential contacts. They also took advantage of the built-in notification system within the platform, which suggested new contacts and notified them if leads changed roles. By prioritizing certain leads, they could track new opportunities they might not otherwise have found - if a low priority account hired a new CMO who had used Sprinklr at a previous company, this could now be identified as a potential lead and a key opportunity to engage and sell!

Sprinklr has a relatively long sales cycle, but by building a program of regular content, the sales team managed to find ways of legitimately staying connected with prospects and staying front-of-mind - minimizing the risk of being forgotten! Sharing relevant content, solving problems, and answering questions positioned the team as knowledgeable and credible within the industry.

And on top of all of these long-term benefits, the Sprinklr team did make sales, generating commercial return. Their social selling approach increased their average deal size by 10.4%.

Everyone wants to generate leads and make sales, but the commercial value in social selling is so much broader than that - from collecting data to improving efficiency and building relationships.

GETTING STARTED

Sounds pretty convincing so far, right? But before you dive in to social selling, there are a few more points to consider to ensure you're making the right choices. First things first, let us think about your strategy.

Who owns the social selling strategy will often depend on the nature of the business itself and the industry you work in? Some industries are far more active on social media in general, whilst others remain more cautious in their approach. Certain industries and businesses also have tight restrictions on what can and cannot be shared online, so be sure to check what the case is for your own situation before you start posting!

Business size and culture may also prove important factors in your social selling strategy - if the business is already using social media for marketing purposes, these activities will shape the types of content you post, as you will likely be re-sharing articles, videos, or opinion pieces. Similarly, it might be worth assessing which platforms and target audiences have, historically, proven the most successful for the marketing team, as there is sure to be some crossover.

If you are part of a large sales team or division, the overall social selling strategy will likely come from a sales leader or designated senior team member - someone who can ensure that the activity and approach aligns with wider business goals. These will include revenue-based goals such as generating sales leads, but could also be to "help raise the brand of individuals or the overall business."

Whether the approach is top-down or led by individuals, this alignment with key business goals alleviates the risk of wasting valuable time on activities that will not help to support the overall business or that do not deliver value. It can be harder to measure return on investment with social selling - often, conversion can take a long time or can occur some time after an initial connection is made, so it is important to ensure you are approaching social selling in a way that makes sense for your role and your business.

Once you are on the way with your social selling journey, consider how you could help others in your team to get started. In larger teams, this might be a chance to transfer skills, encourage people to work together and learn from each other's successes. You might consider setting up review sessions with colleagues, adding updates to team meetings or setting aside time to show and tell your findings, helping everyone to learn and improve.

Now that you know what you are trying to achieve, it is time to set up a profile! You will likely already have an account on some of the main social platforms, but it is always worth going back and making sure it is optimized for social selling.

Social selling can be a great tool for finding prospective connections, but they need to be able to find you too! Your profile will likely include your job title, particularly on platforms that are more traditionally business-oriented, like LinkedIn.

If your job title is 'Head of Sales,' adding a compelling headline can help to make your role more relatable - something like "Helping businesses drive behavioral change to transform in a digital world." Not only will someone have a higher chance of discovering your profile if they have searched for any of these keywords, but it will also help them understand more about you and what you do.

Your summary is important too. This should expand upon your headline, explaining who your audience is and how you solve their problems with your product or service. Keep it concise - just a few sentences are enough.

Hashtag searching is also common across social media platforms, but it is important to be aware of when and how it is appropriate to use hashtags as part of your profile. By adding relevant tags to content, you share, your posts may appear as trending topics, giving people you are not already connected to the chance to engage with or follow you.

Finally, and it might sound obvious, but a professional profile needs an appropriate photo! This should be up to date and representative of how you look day-to-day. It does not need to be a professional headshot, but should clearly show your face, and you should dress as casually or formally as you would for the office. Consider how you want potential business connections to view you, and use this as a guide.

There are a few last points to consider when setting up a profile for social selling. Some organizations have a policy around the ongoing ownership of your profile and related connections or followers, arguing that because you generated these connections while you worked for them, if you then leave the business, these connections belong to them - not you. This is rare, but it is worth being aware of, and make sure you seek internal advice or guidance on your own company's policy before making any changes to your profile.

Similarly, some organizations have policies surrounding posts on social media relating to the business. Again, it is best to seek specific advice, but often a simple disclaimer stating "These are my own views" can give you the freedom to share your own content and thoughts.

Last, but certainly not least, remember that social media is a public forum. Just as you would not want a client or boss to hear you saying something inappropriate in a meeting or at a conference, the same thinking applies here. It is often difficult to remove something completely online, so it is best to err on the side of caution when using any social network.

That brings us to the end of this first chapter on social selling - next time when we will be looking at the practical side of a social selling strategy and how to measure your activity.

SOCIAL SELLING STRATEGY

We covered the basics of what social selling is, and how to get started, as well as considering the commercial value for businesses operating in today's digital world. We learned that the key to successful social selling is about more than just jumping on Twitter and shouting about your latest products! As with any business endeavor, you will need to have a strategy in place, and a plan for measuring success and optimizing your activity - so that is what we will be exploring today.

REACH

We have made the point before, but one of the most important things to bear in mind when approaching social selling is: it is not a one-time money maker. Rather than using it as a way of directly boosting sales, it is more beneficial to think of it as a chance to build relationships. And we all know that building relationships takes time! That is not to say that you will not find any new leads and end up actually selling to your new connections - it just means you will need to invest some real time and energy.

Whether you are just setting out on your social selling journey, or you have already made headway, you will need to have an understanding of where to reach your audience. This comes from knowing who your target audience is.

Social selling is most prevalent in the B2B world, so recognizing who your buyers are, what they are interested in and where they engage online can really shape your approach.

Just as you would not approach a new contact in person by thrusting a price-list under their nose, it is really no different online. You will want to identify new people with whom you can engage and who may become valuable to you - as buyers, but also as partners, educators, and introducers. This way, you can focus on quality, rather than quantity of effort - and it means you can fit social selling around your other tasks, building it into your working day.

When it comes to first connecting, spend some time creating an introductory message to accompany your follow request. Sending a request with no message or even a generic message comes across like you have not bothered, and can be very off-putting! Try to write a few lines to establish a rapport - maybe you could pose them a question, highlight common connections or reference something they posted that you would like to discuss further. Just like the real world, first impressions matter, so aim to come across as friendly and approachable.

Making connections on social media can be a little like dominoes - once you start, you will of course, have access to the content they share, but the algorithms within the platforms are more likely to suggest related contacts based on these relationships. If you do share a common connection with a potential prospect, this adds a sense of credibility to your own profile and makes prospects much more likely to engage positively with you.

If you are newer to the social media landscape, or have recently changed role or industry, finding leads can seem daunting.

Whatever your situation, when trying to grow your follower-base, avoid the temptation to follow 'just anyone' - you want to make sure these connections will be valuable to you.

But how do you find them?

You could search. All of the main social media platforms have search functions, so whether you are looking for a specific person, a certain organization or even broader areas like job title, industry, or location, searching is a good place to start. And do not feel the need to be too specific here.

Found someone of interest in a part of the world you do not operate? They could still be a valuable contact down the line, introducing you to their own connections or simply sharing your posts to an audience you might not otherwise have reached. Tools like LinkedIn Sales Navigator let you compile Lead Lists, categorized by client, where you can track their activity and easily get in touch if you have something relevant to say.

Even a Google search can be useful for an overview - if a certain keyword brings up relevant profiles on a platform you had not previously considered, that is a useful insight into which platforms might result in the newest connections.

Do not be afraid to use any contacts you have already got - even those in the real world! The nature of your role probably means you spend time with clients and prospects, be that in person or over the phone or email. Make it part of your meeting to-do list to ask questions like, "Where online do you look for industry advice?"

It is always easier if someone opens the door for you, and in a crowded online world, a referral or endorsement from one person to another can go a long way! According to a LinkedIn report, a warm referral increases the odds of a successful sale up to 4 times over, with 70% of B2B companies stating that referrals convert better and close faster than any other type of lead.

Once you have identified where your audience is, it is time to dive deeper into what each platform can offer. It can be tempting to just head straight to platforms that are household names like LinkedIn and Facebook, but having a clear view of your objectives can help you to decide which platforms will work best for your activity. There are a huge number of social platforms available worldwide, and the features of each will often dictate the reasons audiences visit them, as well as the types of content they expect to find there.

LinkedIn bills itself as a "social networking site for business people and professionals to connect", which makes it a great place for extending your network and building credibility. It also has a number of built-in tools, and areas like Groups, which are designed to help users find one another, sparking new conversations.

Twitter has a more personal slant, but that is not a bad thing. People tend to be quite open on Twitter, especially about issues they care about, so if you have something relevant to add to the conversation, this can be a natural and unobtrusive way of doing so. Similarly, once you are comfortable sharing content, you can shape your own Twitter profile, populating it with posts that show off your company, as well as your industry expertise. That way, when it is time to strike up a sales conversation, your contacts will already know your name.

Facebook is by far the largest social media platform, with 9 out of 10 businesses using it. It is however, considered the most personal of the three we have covered, so in order to keep things professional, many companies opt to set up a specific business page, where they can engage with other businesses and suppliers, as well as with their followers.

It may also be worth you looking into more specific platforms or forums used within your industry, as these can provide an opportunity for even more targeted messaging. Whilst they might not have the same volume of users as the big players, a more focused audience with shared interests and concerns could be even more valuable to your social selling activities. Remember, we are interested in the quality of engagement, not necessarily the scale - but you will need to understand your audience.

This will often lead you to forums or groups that you might not have considered, but which could be really valuable to you. You might find that some of these groups are open to members only, and you will need to be approved to join. That is where those first-person connections come in - if they can endorse you or introduce you to the group admin, that is a sure sign that they trust you.

For example, a salesperson who specializes in tech solutions will not have the same success rate on a platform like Mumsnet as someone who sells to brands involved in parenting and childcare. Forums like these are often hotspots for people asking for recommendations and referrals for providers, suppliers, and products, so do not underestimate something just because it is niche.

As always, whichever community you join, be wary of coming across as 'selling too hard.' These forums are great opportunities to listen and learn, so anything that seems too much like a sales pitch can be counterproductive and could even damage your reputation within these groups. Just as when you enter a meeting or networking event for the first time, it is best to act as a respectful guest.

Simply listening into the conversations that are already ongoing will help to raise your confidence if you are feeling a little intimidated, and there is no shame in starting out just liking or sharing a post you think is interesting. In fact, paying close attention to what is being talked about will give you valuable insight on key topics and issues, and it is a chance to assess the tone and see what you could add, shaping your strategy for when you are ready to start sharing your own content.

ENGAGE AND DIFFERENTIATE

Once you have identified how you are going to reach your audience, it is time to think about how you are going to engage with them in these spaces.

The key to successful social selling is to focus less on the 'sell' side, and more on the 'engagement' side. That does not mean it is impossible to see genuine leads appear from your social selling activity; you will just need to keep an eye out for clear signs of intent from the people you engage with. If a prospect asks for a recommendation or gets in touch directly requesting a call, that is great! Often though, it will not be this obvious, so you will need to do a little background work.

Some of the major social platforms have a built-in notification system, allowing you to set alerts for certain keywords or hashtags. This kind of social listening is often used by marketers as a way of understanding how a brand is being talked about online, but it can be useful for salespeople too. If someone posts an article or asks a question relating to a word or phrase you have flagged as important, this could be a great opportunity to get in touch, making you seem relevant and 'diligent.'

You should also make an effort to track any changes to the social media accounts of important clients or prospects - either businesses or individuals. If a prospect of interest changes role, gets promoted or moves employer, sites like LinkedIn are great at highlighting this information. It is 'good social selling practice' to spot these triggers and act on them, setting you apart as someone who's attentive and human, in an environment that can often feel cold and distant. A simple like or a message of 'Good luck' or 'Congratulations' can go a long way - but of course, it is up to you to decide when this is appropriate.

Thanks to the growth of some of the main social media platforms in the last decade, you can learn from great examples of social selling in practice. Not only are there global industry leaders to follow - the likes of Tim Hughes and Jill Rowley are renowned for their expertise on social selling, but every industry will have its own influencers - people who are using social selling to stand out.

There are a number of tools available to help you seek out these influencers, so you can follow and observe them - learning the types of content they share, and when and how they engage with their audience. Beyond this, maybe there is someone closer to home from which you can learn? Who in your network is already active on social media? Perhaps a colleague or a client seems to be 'everywhere' online.

Of course, in reality they are not everywhere - but they do probably have a structured approach to social selling, and maybe even a content calendar to plan when to post good quality, relevant content to their followers. They stand out from the crowd because they have learned to differentiate themselves.

Now that you have gained confidence in social selling, it is time to start acting as a contributor, posting content from your own account. And do not worry - this does not mean writing all of the content yourself! With a good plan in place, you will be doing a mix of creating and curating, sharing third party articles and content from industry publications, news outlets and even re-sharing posts by your own company.

A common fear for those starting out is worrying that they will not know what their audience finds interesting - but if you have taken the time to listen to the conversations that are already happening, you should have some ideas.

Similarly, if the connections you have built up are relevant and worthwhile, and you are posting something that you can relate to, there is a very good chance that they would appreciate it too! It is really no different to any other kind of interaction you might have - if you had read something interesting, would you mention it to one of your connections if you happen to meet them? If the answer's yes, then it is fine to share on a social platform.

Social media is a crowded space, so in order to stand out for the right reasons, you will need to have the right types of content on your profile. The top three most effective content types for B2B are webinars, videos, and blogs - but that does not mean you are limited to just those. Try to match the type of content to the platform you are posting on, and the message you are trying to get across. The specific purpose of your content will vary, but most posts are published with a view to educate, inform, inspire, or entertain.

Educational content is just that - posts which are designed to tell your audience about a broad issue relating to your industry or market. You are not looking to directly reference your business or products here - instead, you are looking to take a stance on a key issue that your audience should know about, and come across as knowledgeable in the process. This will likely take the format of a blog or opinion piece, but you will want a catchy or thought-provoking opener to encourage people to click through and read it. This type of content is particularly successful on business centric sites such as LinkedIn, where users are accustomed to finding long-form content and likely already have an understanding or interest in the topic area.

Content designed to inform takes educational content a step further, and explains how your product or service can offer a solution to those key industry issues. A large percentage of your posts will be informing readers about your employer's offering, so by sharing these, you will also be boosting your company's own content marketing strategy.

We all want to feel inspired, and stories that resonate with your audience will often have high engagement rates. There is no right or wrong format for inspirational content, but for ease of consumption, videos that can be watched within the platform are a great choice for getting a story across - and mean you could explore more visual social platforms like Instagram or Pinterest.

Entertaining content should still be loosely connected to your industry or what you do, but the whole point is to share something which is not necessarily business focused. This could be something fun or even a bit silly; you are looking to engage people and get their attention, and the format is as free as the content - just do not forget to keep it professional.

Try to maintain a balance of content and posts that cover each of these four areas. This way, it will be easier to find relevant third party content to share, and it will help you come across as more rounded to your audience, with a greater chance of being relevant to more of your connections.

By creating and curating a regular feed of high-quality content and posts, you can start to attract attention and build up a following within a community who see you as an expert in your field, or a so-called thought leader. This status can really make a difference to your sales, with 92% of B2B buyers stating that they use social media platforms specifically to engage with thought leaders in their industry.

As you plan which types of content you will post, it is also worth understanding when to post them. This is not just what time of day or what day of the week, but also involves recognizing which types of content will have the greatest impact at different stages along a buyer's journey. Case studies and whitepapers are great for educating and informing a captive, interested audience, but newer leads might respond better to something short-form or visual.

Social selling should be a part of your working practice, but it certainly should not take over and consume all of your time. Once you have identified good, quality content to share, you might opt to use one of the many scheduling tools available.

Many social media managers do not post in real-time on their evenings or weekends and there is no reason for you to do so either!

These tools allow you to create a schedule of posts for the coming weeks or months - although posting month-old content will not do anything to help you seem up to date and in the know, so use these with caution and look to have a balance of planned and spontaneous posts. If you have a wide international audience, you can use these tools to post at a time when most of your followers are online.

MEASUREMENT AND OPTIMIZATION

So, you have identified your audience and set up profiles on the relevant platforms. You have spent time building up some relationships and scheduling posts that you feel are interesting, but without immediate sales to count, how can you measure if your time has been well spent, or if your posts are having the desired impact?

On a day-to-day basis, there are a number of simple areas that you can measure - often, using just the analytics tools provided within the platforms you are using.

It is important to know that your links are encouraging connections to visit your blog or website. Click-through-rate has long been a valued metric not just for social selling, but for digital marketing in general, as it helps you to understand how appealing your content is. It may be that you have a great article, but if your post about it is dull or uninspiring, the rate of people actually clicking on the link will suffer. If you have a range of different content types, it is good to compare the clickthrough-rate for each, to identify the most popular formats.

To measure engagement, you can monitor the likes, comments, and shares you get on individual posts. If certain posts get more engagement than others, you will know they are really resonating with your audience, and you can amend your social selling strategy accordingly.

When measuring engagement rates, do not just focus on your overall number of followers, but the value that those followers provide. 40 followers who regularly engage with what you are sharing and who are interested in the content you promote will be more valuable to you than 400 followers who never engage. After all, your content should help you to move your connections along the buyer's journey, and this will be far easier if they are actively engaging with your posts.

While these metrics are often known as 'vanity' metrics, they are useful to help you ascertain how your followers are engaging with the content you share. You will then be able to use these metrics to develop benchmarks, giving you something to measure future activity against when you try different variations.

If you are just starting out, aim to post a few pieces of content per week and monitor which ones seem to get the best response. Then you can adjust your timings accordingly, whilst increasing the types or frequency as you go.

For a more in-depth look at the return on investment of your social selling activity, you will need to dive into your CRM or sales-management system. As long as you tag or track any opportunities that come in via social, these systems can give you information on how social selling has influenced the value of your sales pipeline, the number of leads it has generated and how much business you have won as a result.

Social selling offers great promise for business - in a global survey by the Miller Heiman Group, 57% of sales leaders said they currently make use of social selling tools, with a further 18% saying they plan to do so in the next 12 months.

With huge potential for growth from social selling, now is the time to get started.

———————— ○ · ● · ○ ————————

PART III

SOCIAL MEDIA IN CHINA

SOCIAL MEDIA IN CHINA

China has a population of over 1.3 billion people, more than any other country, and it is now the second largest economy and importer in the world. As its economy has grown in the past few decades, its middle classes have increased in number from fewer than 300,000 people to more than 400 million - a figure that is expected to grow to over 550 million by 2022.

So, why should this be of interest to you? And what does it have to do with social media? Well, the nation's size and economic development positions it as a marketplace rife with opportunity, and its burgeoning middle class has brought with it a new generation of eager and sophisticated shoppers, whose buying habits are greatly informed, encouraged, and facilitated by social media platforms.

Social media in China operates under a unique landscape influenced by government regulations and cultural preferences. In terms of privacy and platforms

Social media in China is characterized by government regulations and surveillance. Users must register with their real names and national identification numbers, which allows the government to track and monitor online activities. The Chinese government employs strict content censorship, often removing posts that are politically sensitive or deemed inappropriate. Platforms must comply with these regulations and use automated systems and human moderators to filter content. China has implemented laws such as the Personal Information Protection Law (PIPL) and the Cybersecurity Law, which govern how companies collect, store, and process personal data. However, these laws also mandate data sharing with government authorities when requested.

That implies platform practices in terms of data collection. Chinese social media platforms collect extensive user data, including personal information, location data, browsing history, and transaction records. This data is used for targeted advertising, personalized content, and improving platform services. Both the government and platforms can monitor user activities. Platforms may use algorithms to detect sensitive content and report it to authorities. While users have some control over their privacy settings, the extent of this control is limited compared to Western platforms. The pervasive nature of surveillance means users must be cautious about what they share online.

In this section, we will take a look at China's social media landscape: seeing how it differs from what can be found in the West, and how eCommerce is deeply woven into its functionality.

SOCIAL MEDIA & SOCIAL COMMERCE

You will most likely be aware that China has a very different online ecosystem to the West. Facebook and Google - two technology giants that millions of us use every single day - are not available in China, and access to Amazon is becoming increasingly limited, especially since it closed its domestic eCommerce business in July 2019. Instead China has its own technological heavyweights - Baidu, Alibaba and Tencent.

Baidu is the most popular search engine in China, often referred to as 'the Chinese Google.' Alibaba is the world's biggest online commerce company. It owns Tmall - one of the largest online retail websites in the world - and Alipay, which Chinese consumers use every day to make payments online. And Tencent is a corporate titan which owns some of China's most prominent social media platforms and messaging apps including WeChat.

These giants control China's major social media and eCommerce channels and, importantly, whilst social media and eCommerce are often linked in the West, Chinese consumers are accustomed to a more sophisticated integration of the two. Engaging with social media and making online purchases can be viewed as one seamless experience - often within a single application. This interplay between social media and eCommerce, often called 'social commerce,' is a

part of daily life in China that has yet to be widely adopted in the West. Along with social media, retail in China is particularly driven by considerable mobile usage. Over 95% of China's online population use their mobiles to access the internet and over 80% used their mobile phone to shop in 2017 - searching for content, engaging with brands, and purchasing goods and services all within the same applications on their mobile devices.

You could even go as far as saying that many are managing their whole lifestyle through their mobile... from arranging business and leisure activities, to purchasing online goods and paying bills, and even unlocking electric cars, bicycles, and umbrellas for hire.

Let us take Sze-Wing, for example. In a 24-hour period, Sze-Wing will orchestrate her work and play entirely on her mobile device through Chinese social commerce platforms alone. In the morning, she might hail a taxi through DiDi, or, if the weather permits it, hire a shared bike via Mobike, both of which can be accessed through WeChat. At work, she might use WeChat again to take a conference call and send documents without even having to sit down at her desk.

This way, she is less likely to be caught scrolling through her friends posts on Weibo, WeChat and Douyin on company time!

During her lunch break, Sze-Wing catches up on her favorite TV show on Youku and reads recent headlines provided by Toutiao. Once she manages to make it to her desk in the afternoon, she gets on with some research using Baidu search, sharing her interesting insights with the team through a shared drive in Baidupan. After a hard day's work, Sze-Wing kicks back, orders her dinner via Ele.me, and treats herself to some online shopping via Tmall, making sure to look at her friend's product reviews on Xiaohongshu before committing to any purchases.

With consumers managing so many aspects of their lives using their mobile devices, China is increasingly becoming a cashless society, with mobile payment systems being used to pay for almost anything. While in the West, services such as Apple Pay are experiencing a relatively slow uptake, Nielsen research shows that 70% of Chinese consumers have used WeChat Pay, and a staggering 92% have used Alipay. To put this in context, WeChat Pay boasts over 1 billion active monthly users in China alone, whereas Apple Pay has only 127 million worldwide.

Retail spending also differs from that of the West with regards to who the customers are, and what they are buying. In China, consumption is being driven predominantly by the country's Millennials and Generation Z, and they can be characterized by a greater appetite for luxury goods...

Reports show that Chinese consumers buy luxury goods more regularly than those in the West. With an average age of 35, they are also far younger than Western luxury shoppers, 10 years younger in fact. And they are taking advantage of China's rich social media landscape to find what they are looking for...

In 2016, the research company McKinsey interviewed over 10,000 Chinese consumers - between the ages of 18 and 56 - across 44 cities. What they found was that shoppers are becoming more selective about where they spend their money, shifting from mass market to premium goods and services. They also discovered that over 50% of those interviewed were not just looking for 'better' products, they were looking for the best and the most expensive products, many of which are provided by Western brands.

Luxury brands such as Gucci, Alexander McQueen and Hermes are enjoying increasing sales in China, many of which are happening online and cross-border, where shoppers are making purchases having interacted with the brands through their presence on Chinese social media platforms.

But do not be mistaken in thinking that only luxury fashion brands are capable of success in China. Chinese consumers tend to be brand-driven in most of their purchase decisions. Brands such as Tangle Teezer, for example, have enjoyed huge success in China having reached out to audiences through Weibo, along with Starbucks, which has done well to make its presence known through WeChat, encouraging users to share vouchers with their own friends and followers.

We will explore these in more detail, but whether you are selling designer handbags or hairbrushes, what is clear is that Chinese shoppers have a serious appetite for what they consider to be the best, most highly-regarded brands available.

CHINA'S KEY SOCIAL MEDIA PLATFORMS

So now that we understand the context and importance of social media's role in China, it is time to explore the key platforms. It is worth being clear here that there's very little crossover between Western social media users and social media users based in China, so global brands need to have a strategy for each.

For Western brands looking to get a solid foot in the door, establishing a presence on WeChat and Weibo - two of the biggest social media platforms in China - is a great place to start.

WeChat is, at its core, an instant messaging app developed by Tencent. First released in 2011, by 2018 it was one of the world's largest standalone mobile apps with over 1 billion monthly active users.

It is often likened to WhatsApp, but WeChat is much more than just an instant messaging app. It is also a social media platform and a mobile payment application, connecting Chinese consumers to almost everything. Forbes describes it as one of the world's most powerful applications because it has so many functions, allowing other apps and brands to integrate their own content and services. And as we have seen, social apps like WeChat go far beyond traditional social media functionality, catering to all aspects of daily life.

Brands have the opportunity to create WeChat Mini Programs, bespoke low memory apps embedded within the platform, furnished with multiple functions to drive brand awareness and engagement, and sell to users. Within these Mini Programs, brands can host multimedia content, live stream, and sell products using the "See now, buy now" feature. WeChat has made the process of setting up these apps so simple that brands can get their campaigns onto the platform within just three weeks.

Now let us take a look at Sina Weibo. Usually referred to simply as 'Weibo,' it is a microblogging platform with almost 500 million monthly active users, so it is definitely worth your attention...

Weibo tends to be viewed as the Chinese equivalent of Twitter. But since its launch in 2009, its functionality has developed to the point that this comparison does not really do it justice. In fact, it operates much more like a combination of Twitter, YouTube, Facebook, and Instagram....

Mirroring Western social media platforms, it allows direct comments and conversations between brands and consumers. Users can "follow" people and official brand accounts, as well as generate their own content in various forms, like posts and articles containing photos, videos, and links to products on online retail platforms. On top of this, it also allows brands to display product catalogues to users, and offers a variety of paid advertising opportunities such as 'fan headlines,' which allows brands to pin their post or account to the top of their followers - or prospective followers - feeds.

Weibo is also the main source of news for many Chinese people, and with its formidable user base and vast body of user generated content, it is essentially an enormous searchable database. In fact, one of its popular features lists the most searched hashtags, making it an effective source for online users to find out the hottest discussions in China.

It is worth pointing out that Weibo is an open and public platform, which makes it an ideal way for Western brands to gain immediate exposure and reach new audiences. And here's some more good news: Weibo can also be viewed in English, which means there is very little stopping you from familiarizing yourself with it right away.

Alongside WeChat and Weibo, there are many other social media platforms enjoying rapid growth in China. Two in particular that have risen quickly through the ranks are Douyin and Xiaohongshu.

Douyin, known as 'TikTok' outside of China, was launched in 2016 and encourages its users to shoot short video clips, edit them with various special effects and music, and share them. If you were to try to draw a comparison, it would likely sit somewhere between YouTube and Snapchat. Douyin can be a really fun way for brands to encourage audiences to interact with them, and this did not go unnoticed by Michael Kors, one of the first luxury brands to partner with Douyin, who, after just a week witnessed over 30,000 users creating their own content related to the brand.

Douyin is just one example of how quickly new Chinese social media platforms can emerge and grow. The product itself was developed in just 200 days, and it now enjoys over 150 million daily active users. So, for brands looking to develop an effective social media strategy in China, keeping a close eye on the latest developments and changes to functionality on platforms is essential...

Xiaohongshu, also known as Little Red Book or 'RED,' is best explained to a Western audience as a hybrid of Instagram and Pinterest, with eCommerce functionality seamlessly combined. Over 30 million monthly active users share their own content about travel, fashion, beauty, parenting, music, food, and much more, while other users respond with comments and likes.

All this original user generated content, a 'Nearby' feature allowing users to explore content that is locally-relevant to them, and the ability to categorize and search through posts using hashtags... all combine to form a kind of search engine - or dynamic recommendation tool - for product discovery.

Many celebrities are very active on RED, and whilst on Weibo they might share their points of views and talk about recent public events, on RED they tend to share their beauty secrets or other lifestyle recommendations. This gives brands the opportunity to work with them and promote their products. Some of RED's most popular accounts boast millions of followers, and it is not uncommon for the products they recommend selling out soon after they've posted.

In addition to social sharing, RED also offers cross-border eCommerce functionality, selling fashion and beauty products from around the world. Audiences often find these products through reviews from influencers within the platform. And having bought the product, customers will often go on to share their own reviews, contributing towards further awareness and sales.

Whilst we are on the topic of influencers, be sure to note that they are not just found on RED. Influencers can be found populating the entirety of China's social commerce landscape, and they will likely play a significant role in your journey to business success...

SOCIAL IN CHINA – KEY THEMES AND TRENDS

Influencers are individuals who have a large enough following and a level of perceived authority such that they are able to have a significant impact on consumer preferences and decision-making. Brands often work with them to drive brand awareness and sales and - just as this form of marketing is established in the West - it is also ingrained within Chinese social commerce. In China, however, they go by a different name - Key Opinion Leaders...

To be recognized as a Key Opinion Leader, or 'KOL' for short, influencers need to have more than 10,000 followers. There are three broad categories of Key Opinion Leader - experts, celebrities, and Wang Hong. Wang Hong are essentially those who have reached a kind of celebrity status through their prominent online presence. In the West, their closest equivalents are internet celebrities or social media stars like Zoella and Tyler Oakley. Wang Hong, and other Key Opinion Leaders, often have large and dedicated fan bases - which make them suited for the job - and their influence on audiences will only increase for the foreseeable future, so they are vital to the success of any brand looking to do business in China.

In China, compared to the West, traditional advertising and promotions tend not to be the focal point of strategic planning. Instead, campaigns are devised around Key Opinion Leaders because they are proven to be more effective in influencing online purchases and driving brand awareness... and they can often do so at a lower cost than traditional advertising. This is something that brands such as Louis Vuitton and Nike are well aware of; both of them having employed Key Opinion Leaders to great success.

The increasing importance of Key Opinion Leaders has led Weibo to create a standalone marketing platform called 'Micro-tasks,' in order to control how content is shared, and as a way of taking a slice of the vast revenue that Key Opinion Leaders can generate. Creative content needs to be approved through this platform before going live, and Weibo then takes a commission.

A word of warning, however: just as in the West, there can be fake influencers - those who buy followers rather than developing genuine audiences - and brands are not going to benefit from working with them. For established brands, this risk can be mitigated by entering into a legal agreement with the Key Opinion Leader. This way, brands can better understand how much traction they are getting when they post on social media.

Now we have a good idea of the role and impact that Key Opinion Leaders can have for your business, it is worth pointing out that the power of their voice, and the collective voice of social commerce as a whole, can seriously harm your efforts if your business fails to conduct itself in an acceptable way, or fails to respect local culture.

One Western brand that found themselves in hot water was Dolce & Gabbana following a misguided video campaign introducing its first fashion show in China. The campaign was heavily criticized for its cultural insensitivity and the hashtag #dgdesigner began trending on Weibo for all the wrong reasons, with influential Chinese celebrities publicly stating that they were going to boycott the brand, and existing customers sharing footage of themselves destroying items they had previously purchased.

As a result, Dolce & Gabbana was forced to cancel its first runway show in Shanghai, and Chinese eCommerce platforms such as TMall, JD.com and Secoo removed their product listings. Needless to say, this should prompt you to think very carefully about how your messaging might be received by Chinese audiences.

Before we finish, there are a few more things you need to be aware of before getting started. First of all, social media in China is not an appropriate platform for users to discuss politics - as they often are in the West. So, be sure to steer clear of sensitive political debates, otherwise, your content might be deleted, and your account could be frozen.

Secondly, Chinese social media users are not quite as diligent when it comes to avoiding copyright infringements. So be aware that your official images and videos may well be re-used without prior permission.

On a related note, whilst GDPR in Europe has become a hot topic, China does not yet have this kind of data protection regulation in place. But this may not be the case for too long. For instance, the Chinese Consumers Association is beginning to urge for changes to be made after finding out that 91% of the mobile apps they researched were holding too much personal information around location, contacts, identities, and phone numbers.

And finally, it is worth bearing in mind that sharing content across different platforms is not as straightforward as brands will be accustomed to in the West - sharing a YouTube video on Facebook, for example. Different Chinese social media channels - and the corporations that own them - want to keep control of their own platforms and the content on them. This is not to say it is impossible, it is just something you will need to get to grips with along the way.

SOCIAL MEDIA STRATEGY IN CHINA

We explored China's social media landscape and how it differs from what can be found in the West. We also discussed 'social commerce': how eCommerce is deeply woven into social media's functionality, and how the buying habits of Chinese consumers are greatly informed, encouraged, and enabled by social media platforms and the Key Opinion Leaders that use them. Without a shadow of a doubt, social media can often be instrumental to achieving business success in China. Now you have been acquainted with the key players and trends, we will take a look at social media in action, visiting examples of how it is been used by Western brands to capture the attention - and even the hearts - of Chinese audiences on their home turf.

Global brands that have enjoyed notable success in China have carefully observed the cultural differences between them and their new audiences, not just distinguishing between languages, but also respecting the tendencies and sensitivities of Chinese consumers. In fact, many brands collaborate with specialist agencies who provide expertise in this area, working together to create and maintain social media accounts and develop specific campaigns, especially when they are just getting started in China.

PROMOTION & SELLING PRODUCTS

Consumers in China regularly engage in 'social commerce,' which combines social media and eCommerce in one highly integrated experience. Every day, and often within a single platform, social media will facilitate the entire process of purchasing goods and services.

WeChat is a great example of this. It is not just an instant messaging app, it is also a social media platform and a mobile payment application, connecting Chinese consumers to almost everything. And so, companies looking to succeed in China should employ social media as their top sales tool, which not only creates demand, but also closes the deal...

One of the key benefits of WeChat is that it allows brands to create Mini Programs - bespoke apps within the platform that host a variety of content and calls to action. British high fashion brand, Burberry, developed a Mini

Program to effectively drive sales in China, launching a flash sale event on WeChat immediately following the catwalk show for its Spring/Summer 2019 collection. 25 of the items exhibited on that day - ranging from their signature trench coats to t-shirts and sneakers - were made available to purchase for 24 hours.

But here is the thing: participation in Burberry's flash sale was invitation-only, restricted to users of its WeChat Mini Program. To create a buzz before the big show and the flash sale to follow, Burberry also gave these Mini Program users a sneak peak of what was to come - revealing their new logo and a black monogram t-shirt.

This 'social first' strategy seems to have done the trick, as nearly half of the products were sold out before the end of the sale. By allowing flash sale access only to those who had opted in to its Mini Program, Burberry created an incentive for customers to do so. This was instrumental to the success of the brands sale, because from here, Burberry could retarget opted-in users with news about the forthcoming collection. This inevitably generated anticipation and a deeper engagement surrounding the products Burberry had on offer, and ultimately, led to direct product sales, which, by no coincidence, took place within the very same platform.

Another Western brand that is utilized social media to boost sales - proving that it is not just high-end fashion brands who can achieve success in China - is Tangle Teezer.

Shaun Pulfrey, the inventor of the Tangle Teezer hairbrush, had always intended his company to go global. Yet, it was still unexpected when, one day, the company's website began to receive thousands of orders from China after word began to spread on the country's online platforms that the famous supermodel, Liu Wen, was a big fan of her new Tangle Teezer hairbrush.

While the brand's initial success with Chinese audiences could be considered a stroke of luck, Tangle Teezer immediately took advantage of its good fortune. It approached TMall.com, one of China's largest online marketplaces - to get its official brand store up and running, and worked with Hot Pot Digital, a digital marketing agency specializing in China's consumer market. With its help, Tangle Teezer created a presence on several social media platforms, most notably Weibo.

Weibo is an open and public forum for discussion with a mass of user generated content, essentially making it an enormous searchable database. By establishing itself here, Tangle Teezer could promote the quality and cutting-edge design of its products, and direct its followers to purchase. As a result, China became one of the brand's biggest international markets.

Along with WeChat and Weibo, Key Opinion Leaders can have a huge impact on consumer decision-making and brand success in China. Boasting more than 10,000 followers, and a perceived authority to match, they are proven to be more effective in influencing online purchases than traditional advertising, and often at a lower cost.

This is by no means a closely guarded secret, and it is common for brands to partner up with Key Opinion Leaders to help win the hearts of Chinese consumers. But, while some brands might settle with asking influencers to simply mention them in a social media post or pose next to their products, other brands go above and beyond... In 2014, multinational clothing company H&M and world-famous fashion designer Alexander Wang collaborated to design a collection of 61 new products. To make sure they would be bought by China's fashion-loving shoppers, the launch of the range was supported by a social media campaign that harnessed the powerful influence of Key Opinion Leaders.

H&M selected a number of Key Opinion Leaders, including fashion editors, bloggers, and celebrities, all of whom were well suited to endorse the brand's value to fan bases that were perfectly matched with H&M's desired audiences. From here, H&M went all out, inviting its Key Opinion Leaders to live broadcast a massive party it had thrown in Shanghai using the hashtag 'WangisComing' on both Weibo and WeChat.

Many high-profile celebrities attended, some of China's most popular performers graced the stage, and even Alexander Wang himself was the life of the party, dancing with guests and launching merchandise into the crowd, so it is no surprise that the hashtag began trending on Chinese social media.

By the time the collection was released in stores and online, it was so popular with Chinese shoppers that the official H&M eCommerce site went down, and once it was back up and running, the collection was completely sold out...

It is clear to see that the careful selection and implementation of Key Opinion Leaders was the bedrock of H&M's campaign success, not only working to target its ideal audiences, but also creating an event that would generate genuine excitement from influencers.

The brand put on a show that was actually engaging, and consumers noticed, fueling a pre-buzz around the new collection release that was reflected in the popularity of its hashtag, a hashtag which not only further spread the word, but also helped to track engagement across social media.

BUILDING BRAND COMMUNITIES

Social media in China is a great way of driving awareness and purchases, but there is more to business success than completing sales. Cultivating your brand, and how consumers perceive it, is also hugely important. This is especially true of

Chinese consumers, who are particularly brand-driven in their purchase decisions. Chinese shoppers often favor brands that are considered to be 'the best,' so it is vital that brands work to be regarded as such. It is not just about the price tag or the status attached to their products: companies also need to use social media to build a genuine sense of community around their brand...

One of the finest examples of brand building in China is provided by the London Rubber Company, Durex. When it first registered an account with Weibo in January of 2011, Durex only used its profile to present its latest products and share ads. But it did not take long for it to realize that to increase brand equity in China, forging strong relationships with new audiences was essential.

Durex began using Weibo to initiate conversations on dating and marriage, encouraging followers to comment and get involved. Due to the nature of its product, Durex often communicated in a deliberately indirect or ambiguous way, leaving readers to fill in the gaps and discuss the true meaning of its posts, and these online threads frequently became trending topics on Weibo.

Durex even developed its own special brand mascot on Chinese social media – a playful fictional character called "Little Du Du" - who is well known for providing sexual health information and engaging in humorous - often highly personalized - back and forth dialogue with other users.

Essentially, Durex focused less on pushing their products and brand, and concentrated more on forming real connections with their audience online.

After a well-known blogger wrote a post about an argument they had with their girlfriend, Durex sent flowers and a box of branded condoms to cheer them up. The blogger wasted no time in proudly posting a picture of Durex's act of kindness, which went on to be shared widely amongst and beyond their 300,000 followers.

Durex encountered some unique challenges when it came to generating interest in China. Firstly, there was only a small market for what they offered. With only one in ten sexually active Chinese people using condoms, Durex's task was not only to familiarize China with their brand, but also to create a market for their product.

Secondly, Durex had to build a rapport and sense of community with consumers in a culturally-relevant way.

By providing valuable sexual health information, opening up lighthearted discussions about relationships and romance, and working to cultivate real relationships with other Weibo users in highly creative and personal ways, Durex managed to effectively popularize their product and build significant online brand loyalty whilst respecting local sensitivities.

As a result, Durex is now generally one of China's most loved brands on social media, and boasts over 3 million followers on Weibo alone. But there is still work to be done. Relationships are an ongoing process, and if it wants to remain in favor with its audiences, Durex will need to continue to engage with them in a considerate and discerning way.

Starbucks also had a tough challenge to face when it came to creating a following in China. The coffee house chain had big plans when it entered the market, aiming to have 6000 stores open in mainland China by 2022 - the equivalent of opening a new store every 15 hours! But the real challenge it set itself was filling all of these stores with customers, so it needed to build its brand community in China just as quickly.

One way it did this was by setting up a fully integrated WeChat Mini Program offering its opted-in audiences exclusive vouchers that they could then share with their friends through the app. Vouchers are a great way to win over new customers, but by offering them exclusively to opted-in Mini Program users, Starbucks is creating an incentive for customers to make the brand a bigger part of their social media habits.

Starbucks also worked with WeChat to co-create an innovative 'Say it with Starbucks' feature on the platform, conveniently enabling users to gift Starbucks products to friends and family. Social gifting is big in China, especially around the Chinese New Year period, so this was a great way for Starbucks to embed itself further into contemporary Chinese culture and the everyday lives and relationships of their new audiences.

We have already discussed Key Opinion Leaders and their capacity to promote and sell products, but it is also worth recognizing that, if you work with them effectively, their large and dedicated fan bases could become yours...

Costing around half the price of the Adidas Originals range, Adidas NEO looked to draw the attention of China's 14-19-year-old. Enter Jackson Yi. Singer, dancer, actor, and one third of TFBoys - arguably the most successful boy band in China - Jackson Yi is important amongst China's youth, and he is also one of the country's most influential Key Opinion Leaders! To better reach out to its key demographic, Adidas NEO appointed him as an 'International Youth Creative Ambassador.'

Once his affiliation with the brand became known, Jackson Yi's fans began to buy whatever Adidas NEO had to offer. But perhaps more importantly, beyond prompting immediate sales, Jackson Yi helped the brand to generate long lasting brand awareness.

One of the ways he did this was through his involvement in promoting the 'Jackson Yi Gift Box,' a special prize awarded to the 1,128 winners of a draw that took place on the Adidas NEO online store. Why 1,128 in particular? Well, because Jackson Yi's birthday lands on November 28th.

As part of this campaign, Adidas NEO used Weibo to launch a hashtag, which the winners did not hesitate in sharing and interacting with when posting photos with their own prizes. These pictures were then collected into an exclusive Jackson Yi poster, which was published online and made available in Adidas NEO stores, incorporating fans as a core part of the campaign.

So, Adidas NEO identified the audience it wanted to connect with, and having done its research, recognized that bringing Jackson Yi into the fold would really help them on their way.

Adidas NEO encouraged fans to act as micro-influencers, playing an instrumental role in spreading the brand's message amongst their network of friends, who in turn would spread it amongst theirs.

By giving out gift boxes - which were of course fully branded, releasing a poster that fans could actually feature in, and launching the topic on Weibo - which ranked third among the trending topics that day - Adidas NEO gave users a great reason to talk about the brand and championed a means of doing so.

MEASURING SUCCESS

As we have just seen, businesses that effectively leverage social media to foster closer relationships with users and increase sales can be generously rewarded for their efforts, but understanding how to judge if campaigns are effective is key to long term success. So, what tools are available to help brands make sense of this?

Both Weibo and WeChat have account dashboards that allow brands to learn more about their users. The data they show, which can be viewed as weekly or monthly sets, can provide brands with insight regarding follower growth and engagement - through reporting page or post views and the quantity of shares and likes.

Although these dashboards might seem daunting to Western brands, there are a number of tools, like Kawo, emerging to help English-speaking client's access and interpret the data they provide.

Once a brand launches its official WeChat subscription account and starts actively posting, it has access to monthly campaign reports that track sales data and disclose valuable data about its users...

The data that WeChat reporting shows allows official subscription accounts to keep track of: how much each post is read and shared, new user subscriptions and unsubscribes following every post, and how users discovered the brand account in the first place. Perhaps the user discovered the brand through their brand URL - known as 'name cards' in this context - or a QR code, which are distributed and used far more prolifically by consumers in China than those in the West.

Demographic information like gender, language, and location, is also disclosed to WeChat subscription account owners, along with interaction data, which tells brands which elements of their account are receiving the most engagement.

This helps brands to understand the users that are showing an interest and in what ways - insight which will be invaluable when it comes to future decision-making.

Moving on from WeChat, Weibo's account dashboards can also provide brands with insight regarding follower profiles, growth, and engagement. They can track changes in a brand's follower count - whether that is weekly, monthly or during specific times and events - and they display a number of graphs showing the volume of post views, comments, likes and shares over a variety of timescales. Premium accounts can also analyze things like their users' ages, registered cities, and interests.

On top of all this, Weibo helps brands to scrutinize the success of their branded hashtags too, tracking users who join the campaign from a branded hashtag through the hashtag profile page.

Of course, specific user engagement figures - whether that is follower count, post readership, or any other seemingly objective indicator - offer a worthwhile perspective for any brand looking to be successful online. But there's more to it than just focusing on metrics...

Numbers are important but relationships matter more, and whilst chasing down follows, reads, shares, and likes might lead to a boost in user interactions with your brand, they are only one side of a complex picture, they are not the be-all and end-all. If you spend time on social media, think about some of the accounts you follow, and the things you find yourself liking and commenting on. It is likely that at least some of those interactions are fleeting, and you forget about them as soon as you have scrolled on, right?

So, if you want long-term success and you are looking to become a household name, it is far more important to cultivate real and meaningful relationships with your audiences. Unfortunately, building this authentic kind of brand community does take time and effort, and it might be difficult to recognize a tangible return from the work you have been putting in.

This is something that Durex's marketing team in China is only too aware of. In fact, when asked how they measured return on investment on social media, they had a very simple answer: "We do not." For Durex, it is impossible. A successful social media strategy is about friendship - something that does not have a dedicated dial or graph on any account dashboard.

Obviously, you are in business to make money, and the fundamental motivation behind using social media is to help you do this more effectively, but do not let this get in between you and your customers. If your brand truly commits itself to making real connections and constructing genuine relationships, you will likely strengthen your market share in China.

GLOSSARY

Brand Awareness is a common and very broad goal within social media, which aims to increase the extent in which people recognize a given brand.

Business-To-Business (B2B) is a selling model in which businesses provide products and services to other businesses.

Business-To-Consumer (B2C) is a selling model in which a business sells directly to consumers.

Consumer-To-Consumer (C2C) is a selling model in which a consumer can sell to another consumer, e.g., when using eBay's marketplace.

Conversion Rate refers to the percentage of visitors who complete a desired action out of the total number of visitors who had the opportunity to do so.

Curating In social media terms, curating refers to finding and forwarding content created by others.

Customer Acquisition is a common goal within social media, which aims to increase new business leads and prospective customers.

Customer Loyalty is a common goal within social media, which aims to increase repeat custom.

Dark Social refers to the wide scale sharing of social content that cannot be captured by web analytics, such as sharing through messaging services like WhatsApp.

General Data Protection Regulation (GDPR) General Data Protection Regulation (GDPR) refers to the EU regulation intending to strengthen consumer data protection.

Hashtag is a designator (in the form of the hash sign or '#') in front of a term that makes it searchable on certain online platforms, for example Twitter or Instagram.

Influencers are people who have the ability to reach others with compelling information, often with the power to sway public opinion.

Social Commerce is the sophisticated integration of social media and eCommerce, to the extent where engaging with social media and making online purchases can be viewed as one seamless experience – often within a single application.

Social Intelligence Social intelligence is the practice of using social media to gather business insights that are applicable across the entire organization.

User-Generated Content (UGC) User-generated content or 'UGC' refers to content that is created by users that can be uploaded to the web for the purpose of consumption, sharing, criticism, or collaboration.

ABOUT JULIAN DELPHIKI

Julian Delphiki is a pseudonym, created to safeguard the integrity of his personal identity and ensure that the focus remains on transformative ideas rather than the individual. This philosophical stance permeates every aspect of his work, from his senior role in a renowned multinational company to his more private collaborations such as one-on-one executive coaching sessions.

For more than two decades, Julian has successfully navigated demanding environments in both well-established corporations and cutting-edge startups in pioneering eCommerce sectors such as fashion. This extensive journey has shaped him into a multifaceted professional whose expertise is not merely theoretical but firmly rooted in practical application. As a seasoned professional, he has honed his skills across diverse functions—ranging from managing complex projects to leadership and activation—consistently delivering results that reflect his unwavering commitment to the success of every initiative.

His strategic vision and adaptability have made him a pragmatic visionary, capable of understanding the needs of the market, businesses, and audiences alike. Beyond his corporate career, Julian is the founder and principal consultant of his own firm, where he channels this experience to help organizations of all kinds optimize their operations and achieve sustainable growth. His work in this space often spans digital marketing, online business, and, more broadly, business management and productivity.

Yet Julian's influence extends far beyond the executive committee. He is also a prominent figure in the realms of personal development and philosophical exploration. As a lecturer in various universities and business schools, he is also a dedicated coach, devoting his energy and passion to fostering personal growth. His coaching philosophy embraces a holistic approach, carefully intertwining personal development with philosophical introspection. This dual perspective enables him to delve deeply into the nuances of critical issues in the social sciences. With a genuine passion for empowering individuals to reach their fullest potential, Julian engages in inspirational and transformative conversations while offering practical tools to catalyze positive change in people's lives.

The fusion of Julian Delphiki's professional and personal spheres creates a truly unique mosaic of skills, knowledge, and a profound commitment to enhancing individuals, organizations, and society as a whole. His ability to bridge the strategic demands of the professional world with the deep self-knowledge required for personal growth provides an extraordinary lens through which to understand human behavior and psychology, the direction of businesses, and the evolution of society.

This interdisciplinary foundation makes him a compelling voice, capable of publishing thought-provoking books on a wide range of topics—united by his core mission of fostering growth and understanding in a complex world.

○ · ◉ · ○

OTHER BOOKS BY THE AUTHOR

La abolición del trabajo. BLACK, BOB and DELPHIKI, JULIAN. 2024.

Maestros del hábito. DELPHIKI, JULIAN. 2023.

Modern philosophers. DELPHIKI, JULIAN. 2022

A modern hero. DELPHIKI, JULIAN. 2022.

Folkhorror volume I. DELPHIKI, JULIAN. 2022.

Ad tech and programmatic. DELPHIKI, JULIAN. 2020.

eCommerce 360. English edition. DELPHIKI, JULIAN. 2020.

eCommerce 360. Spanish edition. DELPHIKI, JULIAN. 2020.

Content marketing and online video marketing. DELPHIKI, JULIAN. 2020.

Digital transformation. DELPHIKI, JULIAN. 2020.

Optimizing SEO and paid search fundamentals. DELPHIKI, JULIAN. 2020.

Social media business. DELPHIKI, JULIAN. 2020.

Tales of horror and history. DELPHIKI, JULIAN. 2020.

Web Analytics and Big Data. English edition. DELPHIKI, JULIAN. 2020.

Analítica web y móvil. Spanish edition. DELPHIKI, JULIAN. 2019.

www.ingramcontent.com/pod-product-compliance
Lightning Source LLC
Chambersburg PA
CBHW070845070326
40690CB00009B/1699